Helion & Company Limited
Unit 8 Amherst Business Centre
Budbrooke Road
Warwick
CV34 5WE
England
Tel. 01926 499 619
Email: info@helion.co.uk
Website: www.helion.co.uk
Twitter: @helionbooks
Visit our blog http://blog.helion.co.uk/

Designed & typeset by Farr out Publications, Wokingham, Berkshire
Cover design Paul Hewitt, Battlefield Design (www.battlefield-design.co.uk)
Printed by Henry Ling Limited, Dorchester, Dorset

ISBN 978-1-913118-67-9

British Library Cataloguing-in-Publication Data
A catalogue record for this book is available from the British Library

We always welcome receiving book proposals from prospective authors.

CONTENTS

Note: In order to simplify the use of this book, all names, locations and geographic designations are as provided in *The Times World Atlas*, or other traditionally accepted major sources of reference, as of the time of described events.

Abbreviations

AAA	anti-aircraft artillery
AAM	air to air missile
AB	air base
AD	air defence
AFAC	airborne forward air controller
APU	auxiliary power unit
ATMS	automatic tactical management system
CAP	combat air patrol
CAS	close air support
CBU	cluster bomb units
CIA	Central Intelligence Agency (USA)
CO	commanding officer
ČZK	Četa za komandovanje (HQ Squad)
ELINT	electronic intelligence
GBK	Grupa za borbeno komandovanje (Group for Combat Command)
HAS	hardened aircraft shelter
HDA	Hrvatski državni arhiv (Croatian State Archiv)
HQ	Headquarters
IFR	instrumental flying rules
IOC	initial operational capability
JNA	Jugoslovenska Narodna Armija (Yugoslav National Army or Yugoslav People's Army)
JRV i PVO	Jugoslovensko RatNo. Vazduhoplovstvo i Protivvazdušna Odbrana (Yugoslav Air Force and Air Defence, in Serbo-Croatian, also 'RV i PVO')
KPJ	Komunisticka Partija Jugoslavije (Communist Party of Yugoslavia)
L	Lovac (fighter in Serbo-Croatian)
LORAP	Long Range Aerial Panoramic Photography
MANPADs	Man-Portable Air-Defence system
MDAP	Mutual Defense Aid Programme
MJ	Muzej Jugoslavije (Museum of Yugoslavia)
MM	mlazni motor (jet engine, in Serbo-Croatian)
NATO	North Atlantic Treaty Organisation
NCO	Non-commissioned officer
OC	Operations Centre
PRC	People's Republic of China
PSS	Poletno-sletna staza (Main Runway)
PVO	protivvazdušna odbrana (air defence, in Serbo-Croatian)
QRA	quick reaction alert
SAM	surface-to-air missile
SFRJ	Socialisticka Federativna Republika Jugoslavija (Socialist Federal Republic of Jugoslavia)
SIGINT	signals intelligence
TDY	temporary duty
TO BiH	Teritorijalna Odbrana Bosne i Hercegovine (Territorial Defence of Bosnia and Herzegovina)
UN	United Nations
UNPA	United Nations Protected Area
UNPROFOR	United Nations Protection Force
USA	United States of America
USSR	Union of Soviet Socialist Republics
VA	Vojni Arhiv (Military Archive, Belgrade)
VFR	visual flying rules
VTR	Vazduhoplovno-tehnička Radionica (Air Technical Workshop, JRViPVO)
ZNG	Zbor Narodne Garde (Croatian National Guards)

Introduction

The air force of the former Socialist Federal Republic of Yugoslavia (Socialistička Federativna Republika Jugoslavija, SFRJ) – the Jugoslav Air Force and Air Defence Force (Jugoslovensko Ratno. Vazduhoplovstvo i Protivvazdušna Odbrana, JRV i PVO), has had many peculiarities, and played a very unusual role during the Cold War. Originally created during the Second World War, and equipped with British and Soviet combat aircraft, it was subsequently equipped with aircraft provided by the United States of America (USA), then the Union of Soviet Socialist Republics (USSR or Soviet Union), and then with indigenous aircraft and equipment. Correspondingly, it also developed multiple, changeable strategies for the case of war – whether with the North Atlantic Treaty Organisation (NATO), in the west, or the Soviet Union and its allies of the Warsaw Pact, in the east.

The JRV i PVO was regarded as a strategic tool in maintaining Yugoslav independence from both of the major blocks during the Cold War. Unsurprisingly, it was massively expanded during the 1960s: it received not only hundreds of new combat aircraft and combat support aircraft, but also had most of its major air bases massively expanded and well-fortified. Moreover, it received a massive – and unique – underground air base (AB) constructed inside a hill outside the town of Bihać, near the geographic centre of the former Yugoslavia.

This AB was constructed close to what is nowadays the international border between the Republic of Croatia and the Republic of Bosnia and Herzegovina: indeed, the boundary runs in between the taxiways and the entrances to the underground facilities.[1] However, while close to the village of Željava, in Croatia, it was administratively subjected to the Bihać garrison of the Yugoslav National Army (Jugoslovenska Narodna Armija, JNA). Therefore, while the entire complex is nowadays often called the 'Željava Air Base' – especially by enthusiasts – it was never known as such while still in operational service. Instead, within the JNA and within the JRV i PVO it was always known as Bihać Air Base.[2]

What made Bihać Air Base worth special attention was the fact that its heart – the '*Objekt*' (object) – was entirely constructed deep inside a hill: in essence, only the taxiways and runways were in the open. In comparison, while a number of other air bases of the JRV i PVO's included underground command and storage facilities, or hardened aircraft shelters made of concrete covered by earth, and the Yugoslavs also constructed a relatively small underground air base outside Pristina, the Objekt was the only permanently used installation of this kind in the former Yugoslavia: for nearly 25 years, from 1968 until 1991, it housed multiple squadrons of Soviet-made MiG-21 interceptors.[3] Indeed, Bihać Air Base was to remain a unique facility well beyond its best times: until today, no comparable air base has ever been constructed anywhere else in western and central Europe. Moreover, the Yugoslav experiences in constructing this facility subsequently exercised strong influence for the emergence of similar installations in a number of other countries, including the People's Republic of China (PRC).

In the following five chapters, this book will describe not only the development of the concept that led to the construction of the Objekt, but also the operational history and routine peace-time operations of the units based there between 1968 and 1991. Moreover, it will provide an operational account during the period of 1991-1992, when Bihać Air Base underwent its major test: operations under the conditions of a civil war.

Bihać: Tito's Underground Air Base is foremost based on preserved archival sources, many of which remain classified and thus not available to most researchers. Moreover, and especially in cases where original sources were lacking, the authors have added the content of multiple interviews with veteran officers and other ranks that served there. Most of the photographs were collected from local archives, museums, and veterans, and have never been published before.

1

Underground Objekt Klek: Early Days, 1958-1968

During the mid-1950s, the top brass of the JRV i PVO (colloquially known as the RV i PVO since 1959) concluded that in the event of a major war – whether against NATO or the Soviet Union and its allies of the Warsaw Pact – its fleet of combat aircraft would require adequate shelters. Already gradually developing, this idea attracted evermore attention by 1958, when the JNA created a new set of defence plans for what it termed the 'whole-scale people's defence war' (*opštenarodna odbrana*). This concept expected that the next war against Yugoslavia was certain to see massive deployment of nuclear weapons of different yields, even on the tactical level, and strongly influenced the training of the JNA and the RV i PVO over the following decade.

Indeed, the longer they observed the developments around them during the following years, the more the Yugoslav military strategists became obsessed with nuclear warfare – to a degree where their only, and logical, conclusion was that they had to construct as many underground facilities as possible in order to protect their forces. The result was the decision to construct extensive underground military installations all over Yugoslavia.

Nowadays, such decisions would certainly prompt an intensive public debate, and raise a number of questions, the first of which would be that of the costs. Underground facilities are always extremely expensive, and thus there would be the question of whether the money invested into such facilities would not have been better spent improving the everyday life of the nation's population. From the standpoint of contemporary Yugoslav military strategists, there was no doubt about this issue: the threat for the state, its independence and sovereignty, its military forces, and the rule of the Yugoslav Communist Party (Komunisticka Partija Jugoslavije, KPJ) was considered to be of higher importance than the care of average citizens. They had to be safeguarded at any price, and the nation's political and military leadership were ready to provide exactly that.

The Idea

Looking back at the related documentation it is impressive to see that the Yugoslav military planners developed and maintained the idea that the JNA should remain capable of continuing to defend the country even after they had been hit by one nuclear weapon. In 1962, they concluded that even the deployment of multiple nuclear weapons against one air base was unlikely to render that air base entirely non-operational. Underground facilities were seen as a sort of a guarantor that this would be the case.[1]

Unsurprisingly, the resulting concepts prompted them into the decision to construct extensive underground facilities and numerous hardened aircraft shelters (HAS), so as to keep the combat aircraft of the RV i PVO safe even from direct attack by nuclear weapons. If such convictions were not enough, they were only bolstered by the experiences from the June 1967 Arab-Israeli War: this not only exposed the vulnerability of any air force operating from bases that lacked hardened protection facilities, but indeed confirmed the entire concept of the whole-scale people's defence war: even if large parts of the country were overrun in a conventional war, underground facilities would safeguard the air force's capability to continue resisting against any kind of aggression.

Certainly enough, as of the 1960s there were only a few large underground facilities operated by air forces, and even fewer meant to protect aircraft – in Europe or anywhere else – and their owners were not the least eager to show such highly classified installations to the representatives of the Yugoslav government led by President (and Marshal of the JNA) Josip Broz 'Tito'. One exception to this rule was the Kingdom of Sweden, a (nominally) neutral country in northern Europe, positioned between NATO-member Norway, neutral Finland, and the USSR. The Swedes allowed the Yugoslavs to examine some of their underground facilities, prompting their visitors into a number of important conclusions about methods of construction, entrance doors with transversal aircraft contours, the distribution and positioning of underground workshops and storage facilities, the practice of towing aircraft into and out of underground installations, and of using nature

The Swedish Air Force's underground facilities deeply impressed the Yugoslavs who later developed their own underground facilities for the RV i PVO. (Author's collection)

to improve the camouflage of the entrances.[2]

Sufficient to say: the Swedish underground facilities deeply impressed the Yugoslavs, driving them to the decision to construct something similar of their own. This was how the idea came into being to construct many of the smaller underground facilities present at all of the major Yugoslav air bases. Indeed the idea for the construction of a major underground air base outside Bihać was also born.

The Idea of an Underground Air Force Base

According to Colonel Dragoslav Sobotka, widely regarded as the 'chief architect' of Bihać AB and the leading designer of several

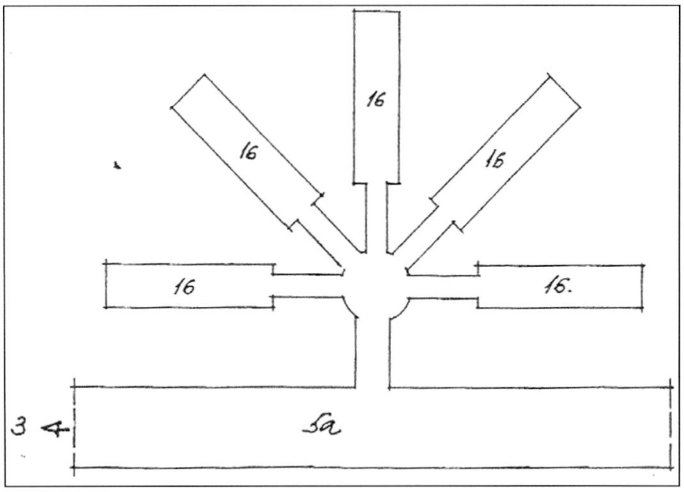

An initial idea for an underground shelter for combat aircraft. (Author's collection)

other underground facilities of the RV I PVO, the related affairs then developed as follows:

> My knowledge about special underground constructions intended for the protection of the air force assets dates back to 1954. I was part of the air delegation headed by the Yugoslav Air Force commander General Ulepič, which visited the Swedish air force. Among others that were shown to us then, we inspected one underground facility of the older type. It facilitated the aircraft with all necessary premises and installations for peace and war-time usage. It had one underground classical reservoir, fuel storages and a Bofors underground arms factory. Moreover, we had talks with their military experts about the different elements of the protection of the underground facilities from the effects of overpressure-waves caused by conventional and nuclear armament.
>
> In 1955 our Air Force HQ created a commission which had to examine technical and tactical facts and figures [for this project]. This marked the start of the programme and the work on the project documentation for one Objekt that would be part of the future underground complex at the airfield near Bihać. I was appointed the chief designer in the Bureau for Special Projects of the Construction Department of the Yugoslav Army [Ministry of National Defence].
>
> The underground Objekt was intended to facilitate two to three reinforced fighter squadrons, with additional space for the overhaul of two aircraft; with needed premises for the headquarters (HQ) of their units, for their pilots, ground crews, technical equipment, armament, fuel, technical- and drinkable water, lavatories and additional source of electric power.
>
> During the work on the main project, the investor [RV i PVO HQ] requested that initially configured Objekts should be expanded through three additional ones. One for the enlarged number of aircraft – one fighter aviation regiment comprised of three to five squadrons, for complete personnel with improvements in comfort – compared with the original project; [Second Objekt] for assets and services needed for maintenance, living, working and combat operations of the fighter aviation regiment in classical or nuclear warfare conditions. It was also to be used as the entry point. [Third Objekt] for the air base ground control and meteorological station, linked – by an elevator – with the interior of the Objekt.[3]

Some documents state that the plans for launching the work on the underground Objekt were supposed to start in 1956-1957.[4] However, the initial planning for the underground Objekt was definitely complete in 1957. It was worked out by the Special Section of the Construction Department of the Yugoslav MND. The underground facility was entitled 'Objekt 505', and designed by two main architects: Colonel Dr Kodelja and Lieutenant-Colonel Smirnov.

The basic idea was that entrances and exits should be kept separated, that the entrance should be single with multiple exits built from both sides, including a spare exit; that the aircraft should arrive at a single point where all the checks would be carried out, and then distributed depending on the aircraft status: if operable – to the galleries left or right – or straight ahead if in need of repairs.

Another important factor was the exit/entrance part of each gallery, which was designed to accept the blast of a massive conventional or nuclear detonation. This was higher and broken in two to three smaller corridors, prior to the armoured door in front of each gallery. The other important factors were ventilation and air conditioning which would enable the constant presence of personnel inside the Objekt.[5]

Before the architects had completed their planning, a suitable location – deep in the Yugoslav interior, and thus estimated as providing extraordinary geostrategic advantages in the case of any aggression – was chosen and the necessary geological research was carried out. The locality in question was a natural plain on the eastern side of Plješevica Mountain, located between the western outskirts of Bihać and the village of Ličko Petrovo Selo. It included a perimeter bounded on the north-eastern side by the village Vedro polje – where the entrance checkpoint was established – and the villages of Klokot, Papari, Musići and Izačić. The south-western side was marked by the slopes of Plješevica Mountain, the villages of Baljevac (which had to be resettled), and Željava (which was inside the perimeter), Ličko Petrovo Selo and Vaganac.[6]

Establishing the 200th Air Base

During the initial period of the construction works on the air base, the Bihać garrison of the RV i PVO included only the 128th Storage Group. This unit was formed in 1953 as the 128th Air Technical Storage [Unit]. Its HQ was in the village of Ripač, south from the town. In 1959, it was reorganised as the 128th Storage Group consisting of the 128th Air Technical Storage in Ripač, and the 455th Fuel Storage in the village of Pokoj. This unit existed until 12 May 1964, when it joined the newly formed air base.[7]

Under the Yugoslav Army's reorganisation plan of 1964, codenamed 'Drvar 2', the 200th Air Base (200. vazduhoplovna baza) was established at the newly-constructed airfield and received the military postal designation VP 4868.[8] Being unique in its structure – because it included an underground Objekt – the 200th Air Base was formed as a 'test' unit. Later the structure was standardised as with other air bases, but the 200th Air Base remained the unique for including 'Objekt Klek' (*klek* meaning juniper berries) and various of its other organisational peculiarities.[9]

Construction Works on the Underground Objekt

The preparation works on the underground Objekt began in late 1957, and the main construction works lasted between 1958 and 1967. Colonel Sobotka continued:

> The Objekt was located in the foothill of Plješevica Mountain, at its eastern side, looking to the city of Bihać. Morphologically it was very convenient since there were natural inlets – which later become entrances – with separating ridges between them. The mountain massif was of crass limestone with lot of cracks, gapes, caves and a lot of natural springs of different intensity. During the

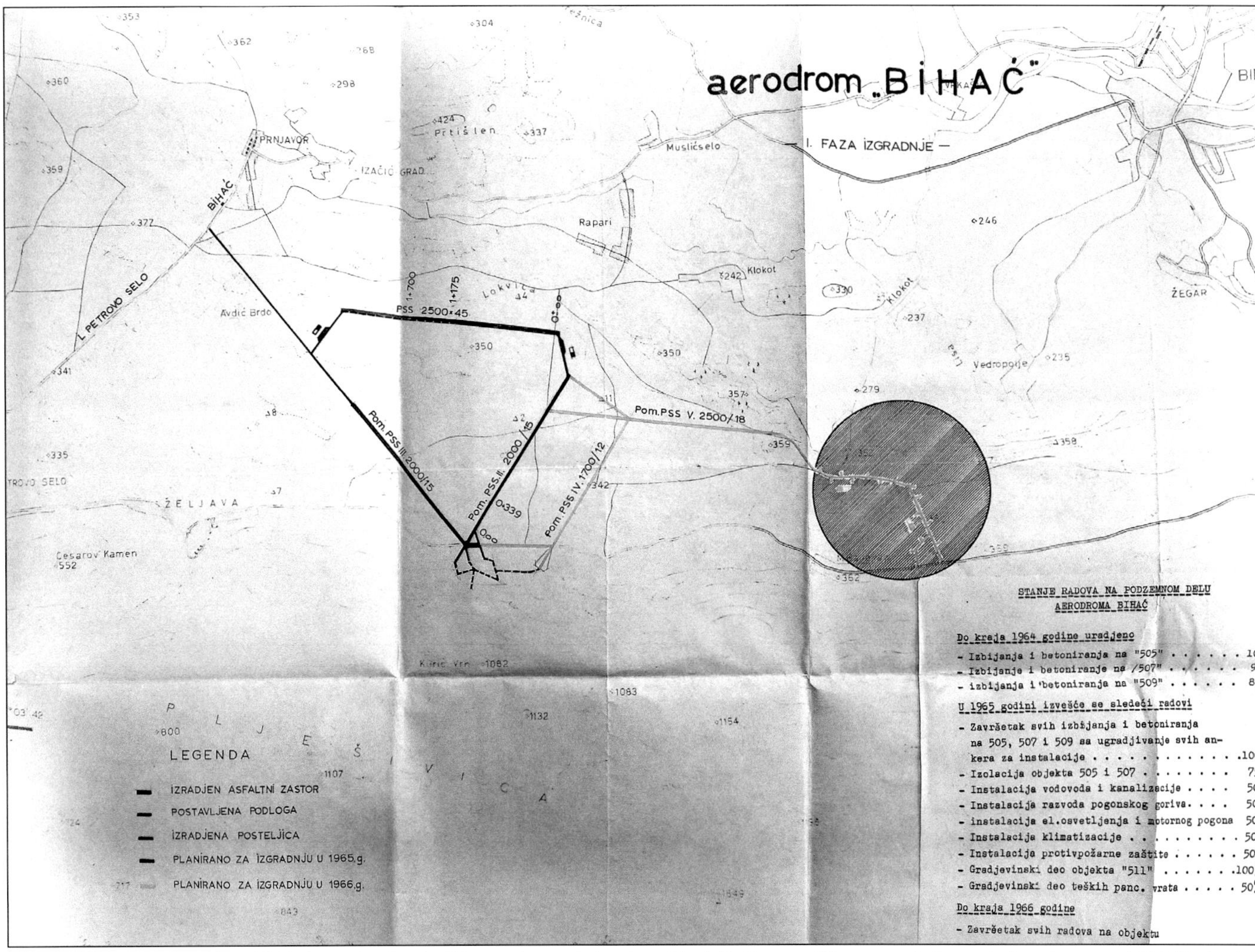

This working map dated late 1964 shows the level of the works carried out on Bihać Air Base and the general disposal of underground Objekts, taxiways, and runways. (VA)

construction works the speleologists were engaged to film the caves in order to bridge them with concrete constructions.

Generally the large caves – some of them 20 metres wide or high – produced the most problems during the construction phase because they had to be over-bridged with concrete elements.[10]

According to orders from 12 May 1958, a special outfit – the 293rd Engineer Detachment (military post No. 4563) – was formed in Bihać. The unit was subordinated directly to the Engineer Department of the Ministry of Defence for the purpose of 'building the aerodrome upon plans developed by the Air Force'.[11] It is likely that this unit was the one which started basic works on the site. Later it would be supported by the much more specialised formations.

During the construction phase, all the facilities at Bihać AB received alpha-numeric code-names such as 505 (main underground Objekt), 507, 509, 511, 808 or Čelopek.[12] Notably, regardless of the extent of construction works undertaken, Bihać Air Base was regarded as 'constructed' or 'ready for use' by 1962, and listed as one of 13 air bases and three 'constructed' aerodromes of the RV i PVO.[13]

All the facilities built outside of the future underground air base were constructed between 1959 and 1964 – mostly by the 293rd Engineer Regiment. In 1964 this unit was replaced by the more specialised 379th Engineer Battalion (Air Force) and Military Construction Enterprise 'Planum'.[14] The 379th Engineer Battalion was established in February 1953 in Zagreb, and subordinated to the HQ V Air Corps. In 1964, the battalion was transferred to the construction site and during the following years undertook all the engineering works at the air base and occasional deployments to other air bases and construction sites.

As such, the 379th Engineer Battalion (Air Force) first worked on entrances K-I and K-II, then on K-III and, finally, on K-IV, which was the last completed. The construction was carried out by the specialised enterprise Soča from Sarajevo. Subsequently, the Military Construction Enterprise Planum from Zemun (near Belgrade) merged with Soča and completed the works. Under the highest level of secrecy, a total of 250 staff worked on the site in three shifts, 24 hours a day, seven days a week.[15]

The most comprehensive task was the construction of the tunnels inside the belly of Plješevica Mountain. As the mountain consisted of extremely firm dolomite rocks, the mining had to be applied extensively. The designers invented a unique system of demolition with 'full and empty charge', which was concluded to be very precise. This system was necessary because of the projected dimensions of the galleries where the airplanes were to be parked: 20 metres wide at the bottom, eight metres high, and over 1,000 metres (1,093 yards) long.

The available documentation shows that all of the underground works on Objekt 505 were completed by 1964. Still, there was a lot of work left to be done elsewhere. It was planned that all digging and concreting works should be finished on all underground facilities in 1965. The other works which were about to start in 1965 were related to water and fuel installations, the electric power network, sewage system, air conditioning and fire protection, and the construction of heavy armoured doors. Contemporary planning envisaged the entire base to be complete by 1966. The map of the site in 1964 shows that extension of runway No. 2 in the direction of the resettled village of Baljevac was planned in the form of a taxiway with HAS and two smaller facilities.[16]

According to the reports from 1968 Objekt Klek was completed and declared operational. The reports from 1969 stated that by the end of year following facilities were also finished:

- Kasarna (barracks; technically approved),
- 505, 507, 509, 511, 808 and 'Čelopek'.

A view from the Objekt to runways No. 3 and 4, with the two main runways in the distance. (MJ)

In 1969, the widening of three taxiways and the building of a water channel between Objekts 'Čelopek' and 'Klek' was finished.[17] The road from the Objekt to the barracks in the village of Željava was finished in 1968-1969 by the 379th Engineer Battalion. The road from the city of Bihać to the air base – via the village of Vedro Polje – was constructed by the 258th Engineer Range (ground forces unit) that arrived from Zagreb.[18] The outside elements of Objekt Klek consisted of the barracks, radar/communication positions and runways. The 200th Air Base's barracks were in the area of the villages of Željava – Ličko Petrovo Selo that were located north-west from the Objekt.

Five Runways

From the very beginning of the operational usage of Bihać Air Base, legend had it that the base had five runways. Actually, there were two main runways (abbreviation 'PSS' in Yugoslav military parlance): one at 142 degrees and another at 322 degrees on the compass, and three runways leading from the 'holes' of the underground Objekt and used for take-offs only.

The first to be covered by asphalt were PSS-3 and PSS-1 in 1964-1965. A map of the site as of that time showed that part of the main runway (PSS-1) and runway No. 3 (which led directly out of the Objekt) were completed by the time. There were still works to be completed on the west side of the main runway though. The map also showed that the works on the aprons and runways No. 4 and "Triangle" which led out from the Objekt would be finished in 1965, and the construction of two other runways (later PSS-2 and No.5) in 1966.[19] Actually, those runways were finished in 1967. Levelling of PSS-1 and its overrun area, then PSS-3 runway sides – safety areas – was carried out in 1968-1969 by the 379th Engineer Battalion.[20] Further extensions – including the overrun areas and stop-ways at PSS-1 and PSS-3, and safety areas for PSS-4, were carried out by the 379th Engineer Battalion and the 333rd Engineer Battalion of the HQ RV i PVO, in 1970.[21]

It is important to note that the names and numbers given to runways and taxiways were different in the project phase than in later usage: originally, there was a single Runway 1 (which remained marked as No. 1), while all others – including the Nos. 2 (later No. 3), 3 (later No. 4), 4 (later No. 5), and 5 (later Runway No. 2) – were considered as 'auxiliary'.

Underground Objekt Klek

Most of the works on the underground Objekt Klek were completed by May 1968, and the base was technically approved for operations. In its final form, the Objekt had three main galleries mutually linked to form a kind of letter M, with one prong to each side and wider middle gallery intended for maintenance and overhaul. Galleries for parking aircraft were 15 metres wide at bottom, some 10 metres high and less towards the ceiling. Crossings between galleries and the entrance sections were increased and higher than the galleries for some two metres. The Objekt had the capacity for 58 aircraft: the intended type to be operational in the Objekt was the Soviet-made MiG-21 and its dimensions were used as the basis for estimation of the space inside the galleries and maintenance area. The other rooms/premises and corridors were between three and 12 metres wide. Engineer Sobotka recalled that the total length of tunnels – galleries and other rooms – was around 3,500 metres:

> All of the living and working conditions for the usage of the Objekt were planned to have full autonomy of 30 days. Electricity, water and drainage network; two reserve diesel electric power-plants, one with 1,000 kVA and the other one with 625 kVA; storage of armament and spare parts, storage with diesel and jet fuel with the distributive installation reaching all of the galleries, space for decontamination of the airplanes, 13 air conditioning chambers with specially protected ventilation shafts, which also acted as the reserve exits on the surface, shafts for polluted air and exhaust from the generators, fuel installations, fire-protecting system, charging stations for aircraft, vehicle and ground system batteries, kitchens with dining facilities, ambulance and sleeping rooms for personnel.
>
> There was a total of 56 different armoured doors inside the Objekt. The wide network for signals inside the Objekt was developed. It was used to monitor, regulate and signal the movements inside and outside the Objekt as well for other needs. The Objekt had a network with loudspeakers linked in 10 "sound circles".
>
> After the trials in Jaroslav Černi Institute, for the first time in Yugoslavia, the Aqua System was adopted for storing the fuel. The 'water pillows' were created in each of five cylindrical steel reservoirs with a capacity of 100 tons of fuel. It was an important step for safety of the Objekt to prevent eventual fire or explosion of the stored fuel inside. The observation post (above the tunnels,

Two runways that led out from the Objekt, left and right with the so-called 'triangle' in the middle, as they appeared in spring 1969 when Marshal Tito visited the base. (MJ)

outside in the mountain) used by the air traffic control had a special steel roof for protection against direct hits from machinegun fire or close range blast of bombs and rocket launchers.

In general, the Objekt was protected from all of the conventional weapon calibres as well as from a ground nuclear explosion up to 20 kT strength. Thanks to the natural configuration of the mountain's foothill the distance between the exit-entrances was projected to avoid the destruction of two at the same time. Special armoured-concrete diaphragms and armoured-concrete gates at the beginning of each gallery were constructed to reduce the pressure of the striking waves at exit-entrance parts of the underground Objekt. They were in separate niches at the [initial] side of the galleries, filled with anti-strike valves, and could be closed by electric power or manually.

Temperature and humidity were ideal. In the aircraft galleries and some of the storages the temperature was reduced to 18c mostly for practical and economical reasons.

Sobotka stressed that during the construction of the Objekt many new construction methods were applied. For the first time the water from the natural springs in the caves, now turned to galleries, was taken, gathered and conveyed through the system of channels bellow the floor construction. Typical for the Socialist Yugoslavia craftsman's mind, Sobotka stressed that of all of the devices embed in the Objekt 'an impressive 95% was made in the local factories of the then SFR Yugoslavia'.[22]

Difficult to Hide

Generally, and as everywhere else in Europe of the Cold War, the Yugoslav armed forces stressed the concept of the 'military secret' and this was the pillar of the everyday work. Nearly everything concerned with quantity and quality – such as the strength, type, location, unit designations, various facts and figures – were declared classified. Unsurprisingly, the constantly growing Bihać AB was regarded as 'above top secret' right from the start of its existence. Intensive works on the site of the new air base required large-scale security measures to prevent any leakage of the classified information.

The 200th Air Base had a Military Police Platoon on its strength from 1964. The military security service also developed a system to control the area and the individuals on the site and in its vicinity. Contact with State Security and local Militia (Police) in the city of Bihać were developed for the same purpose.[23]

No matter the large security measures, the new air base was observed and even photographed from a distance by many of the NATO representatives accredited in Yugoslavia. The Warsaw Pact most likely also took such steps as well, but there is no confirmation of this to date. Twenty three "intrusions" by foreign military and diplomatic representatives prior to arrival of the fighter units at Bihać

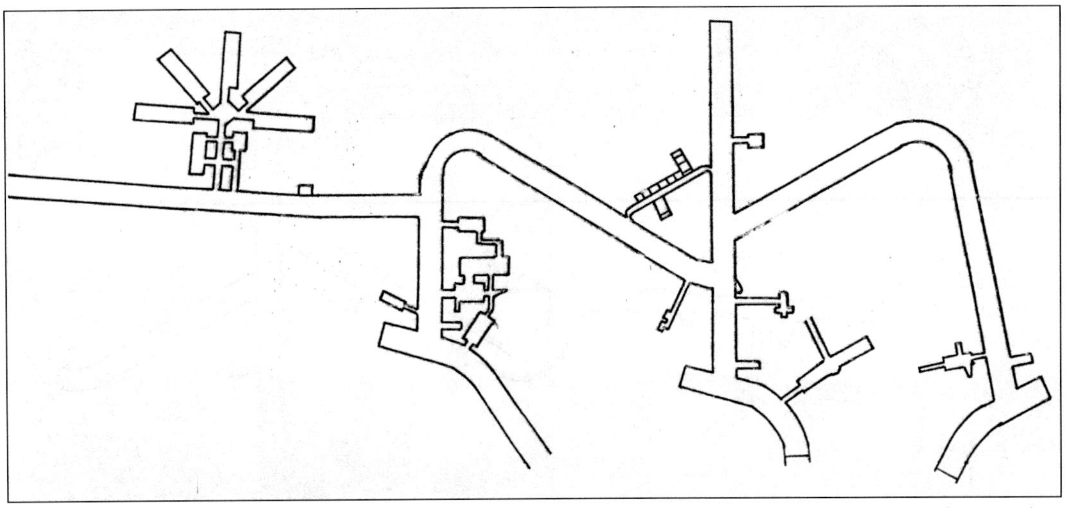

A plan of the galleries and other areas of Objekt Klek, from the manual that each of the active personnel received to get accustomed to the base. (Dušan Buban)

A close look at an inner door with concrete part (top) and the removable armoured protection door (bottom). (HDA)

were noted.[24] The CIA report from Belgrade, written on 17 June 1968 was an excellent example of the interest that the military observers showed in the new air base, it is given in full below:

> Construction at Bihać airfield has been in progress probably since 1959. The airfield has been observed and photographed on several occasions by Western military attaches, who have reported sighting cave entrances and buildings under construction on the side of the Plješevica Mountain, and a taxiway extending from the runway area directly into the mountain. Other intelligence sources have also reported rumours of construction of extensive underground hangars and personnel and maintenance facilities at this airfield.

It is obvious that the new facility attracted the attention of the military-diplomatic representatives in the Yugoslav capital of Belgrade. The US representatives were especially active in trying to discover the progress of the construction works at the site. US defence officials had probably made several trips to the Bihać area, and up to mid-June they concluded following:

> (1) Based on a conversation with a Yugoslav military liaison officer, there is a possibility that MiG aircraft are being stored underground in Yugoslavia...
>
> (2) Natural cave formations in the mountainous region around Bihać could rather easily be made to accommodate a large number of aircraft, and these underground hangars would be protected by almost 5,000 feet of mountain...
>
> (3) Roving security patrols operate in the mountains near the airfield, a security practice not generally followed at other airfields. The extreme measures together with the size of the airfield and long period of construction confirm the importance to the Yugoslav Air Force of this facility.

Such observations managed to discover current status of the air base, most likely prior to the arrival of the MiG-21 equipped 117th Fighter Regiment from Zagreb in late May. It included two serviceable "probable concrete" runways. They were both "connected to an underground aircraft dispersal area consisting of four cave entrances by three taxiways/runways". The reports noted that "an additional cave entrance is connected by road to the southernmost taxiway/runway. A possible air-warning radar facility ... is located 3.1NM SSW of the centre of the longest runway. No large support facilities are observed. The airfield is probably equipped with landing aids."[25]

The enclosed satellite photo imagery of the new Bihać air base also showed the later very distinctive "triangle" apron in front of the underground Objekt and the network of the runways and taxiways. Looking back at this with 50 years of distance, it is almost funny how Yugoslav military representatives created the idea of the secrecy of the base and was typical for Tito's military top brass. They neglected the possibility that its size – visible from the air or space – would give away much detail.

Furthermore, Yugoslav reconnaissance squadrons were ordered not to take any aerial photos of the new air base. One of the former pilots of No. 352 Squadron, Suad Hamzić recalled that in mid-1967, while he was stationed in Pleso-Zagreb and flying in the modified North American IF-86D Sabredog reconnaissance fighters, he was ordered to overfly the new air base. Nevertheless, he was not allowed to take any aerial imagery. Hamzić was ordered to make a low level pass over the base at an altitude over 100 metres just once, and to return back to report and draw a sketch of the runways. He recalls that at this period the story was told among the pilots and other airmen in Zagreb that this was a 'modern, super-secret, indestructible underground Objekt, that everything was prepared just for the war-time, that we shall be deployed there only during the exercises, and that none of the active RV i PVO units will be stationed there'.[26] Ironically, only a year later, Hamzić's squadron converted to MiG-21 fighters and then switched to this new base, where it was to remain for the next 25 years: indeed, Hamzić spent most of his decade-long pilot career there.

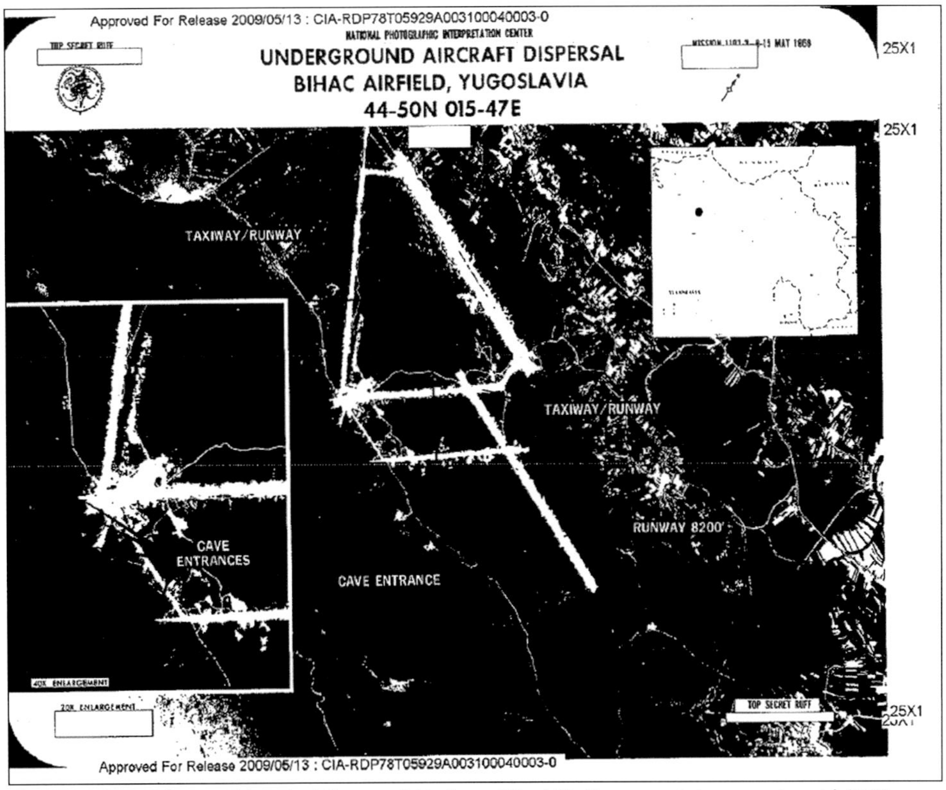

The Yugoslavs did everything that they could to keep Bihać Air Base secret, however in mid-1968 US intelligence had already obtained satellite imagery which revealed at least the above-ground structure of the facility. (CIA/NPIC)

Radar Guidance for the Fighters

Since the mid-1960s and the introduction of Soviet fighters, radars and surface-to-air missiles, the Yugoslav Air Force adopted a Soviet-influenced system of air defence. That system consisted of a joint network including air surveillance, early warning, target acquisition and a reaction with fighters or SAMs. In such a joint system the MiG-21 fighters represented only one part together with the SAM units.

For the core for their air defence system the Yugoslavs obtained Soviet Vazduh-1P (The Air) semi-automated guidance systems in 1967. The system integrated the information gathered from the radar sites and had the possibility of semi-automated data delivery to the interceptors, higher air defence HQs as well as integrating the air-surveillance, fighter and SAM units into the system. Within the fighter aviation it was intended to improve the efficiency of interception in all-weather conditions, day or night. Its components were the ASPD-1, APN-1 Kaskad and Lazur. The Lazur was the data link system fitted to the MiG-21.

Despite the latterly discovered useful position of Plješevica Mountain for a surveillance radar site, in the beginning of its usage Bihać Air Base only had radars intended to support the fighters of the 117th Regiment. The radar unit which was initially deployed to the still incomplete air base was the Četa za komandovanje or ČZK (loosely: the radar company tasked to command or to guide the fighters).

The radar position at Abdića Brdo/k.377 enabled air surveillance and guidance of the fighters from 1968. This photograph shows the Soviet P-12 early warning/surveillance radar at the position. (HDA)

The RV i PVO established two Četa za komandovanje for the support of the MiG-21 fighter regiments with one close to Batajnica air base to support 204th Fighter Regiment, while another one at Kurilovec to support the Zagreb-based 117th Fighter Regiment. The other one would soon be transferred to Bihać, prior to arrival of the first MiG-21s at this base. The ČZK operated surveillance and altitude radars coupled with the Vazduh-1P system. The company at Bihać belonged to the 5th Air Surveillance Regiment with its HQ at Zagreb.

The first radar platoon was ordered to leave for Bihać in 1967. There were no fighter units deployed yet, so it was decided that this period should be used for testing different positions for future radar station deployment. The platoon started with work in August 1967 at the position named Logor-2 (Camp-2) near the main runway No. 1. The company was located in two improvised hangars at the site and was equipped with Soviet P-12 and Yugoslav OAR M-61 surveillance radars and Soviet PRV-11 altitude measuring radar.

When the 117th Fighter Regiment arrived at Bihać, this radar company was moved inside the underground Objekt and additionally equipped with necessary automated guidance and communications equipment. In August 1969, this company was

This photograph shows a Soviet P-35 early warning/long range surveillance radar and a PRV-11 height finding radar at Abdića Brdo/k.377. This site belonged to the 5th Air Surveillance Regiment throughout its operational history. (HDA)

reorganised into two companies: the existing Četa za komandovanje and a new Communications Company.

In 1972, the ČZK Company was re-settled out of the Objekt to a new position in front of the edge of runways Nos. 1 and 4 and was known as Abdića Brdo K.377. At that time, the company was equipped with P-35, P-12 and PRV-11 radars and instrument guidance systems. A Joint Operations Centre was established with the 117th Fighter Regiment in this position in 1975.[27]

2

MiG-21's Nest: 1968-1990

After abandoning of the US sponsored Mutual Defense Aid Programme in 1958 the Yugoslav RV i PVO was in a serious technical crisis until it started to receive Soviet-built MiG-21F-13 fighters in the autumn of 1962. The batch of 41 MiG fighters and 18 two-seaters were used to equip 204th Fighter Regiment at Batajnica Air Base. This was a pivotal base and the most important unit, both responsible for the protection of the capital, Belgrade. When another MiG-21 sub-variant, the PFM, was purchased in 1967, the RV i PVO decided to re-equip the 117th Regiment at Zagreb-Pleso with MiG-21F-13s.

Table 1: RV i PVO's Designations for MiG-21-Aircraft

Original Designation	RV i PVO Designation
MiG-21F-13	L-12
MiG-21U-400 and MiG-21U-600	NL-12
MiG-21PFM	L-14
MiG-21R	L-14i
MiG-21US	NL-14
MiG-21M	L-15
MiG-21MF	L-15M
MiG-21UM	NL-16
MiG-21bis	L-17
MiG-21bis-K	L-17K

The 117th Fighter Regiment had two fighter squadrons (Nos. 124 and 125) equipped with F-86D Sabredog interceptors. In 1968, a third squadron – No. 352 Reconnaissance – joined the regiment. It also operated Sabredogs, but these were the Yugoslav modified reconnaissance version IF-86D with K-24 cameras. The 117th Regiment started conversion on MiG-21F-13 (RV i PVO's designation L-12) in 1967. The regiment reached IOC with No. 125 Squadron after the conversion on the MiGs was held in Batajnica and continued in Pleso. Then, in May 1968, it was ordered to move to a new air base at Bihać.[1]

The first to land at the new air base was No. 125 Fighter Squadron along with part of the HQ and staff of the regiment. The order to move from Zagreb to Bihać was given personally by the RV i PVO Commander General Viktor Bubanj to the new regimental commander Lieutenant Colonel Ilija Zlatić and he was the first to land on a runway at Bihać on 27 May 1968, a day of heavy rain, followed by other pilots from the unit.[2] At that moment, in Batajnica there were two other squadrons of the regiment (Nos. 124 and 352) which were in the late stage of conversion to MiG-21F-13.

Generally, the movement to a remote air base still under construction was quite a shock to many of the personnel who had earlier served at airfields near major cities like Belgrade and Zagreb. The top brass of the RV i PVO thus had a lot to explain, which it did in the course of major meetings – indeed, some of the generals described the service at the Bihać AB as a 'one-year temporary duty'! – even more so once it turned out that the local housing for personnel and their families required lots of improvement.[3]

Czechoslovak Crisis

The sudden eruption of the crisis in Czechoslovakia in late August 1968, when the Warsaw Pact invaded the country, was regarded as the most serious threat to Yugoslavia's independence. Directly from their conversion in Batajnica, two other squadrons of the 117th Regiment with MiG-21F-13s were dispatched to Bihać. Although not yet reaching IOC they were ordered to move immediately to their new home-base at Bihać: No. 352 Squadron took off with its MiG-21F-13s on 26 August. The pilots of No. 124 Squadron were boarded on Douglas C-47 transporters and rushed to Bihać. Later, on 12 September, pilots from Batajnica ferried 12 MiGs and a few two-seaters: the 117th Regiment thus grew in size to 26 MiG-21F-13s and eight two-seat MiG-21Us. The ground crews moved into barracks at the air base: pilots were settled in the 27 July Barracks for ground forces in Bihać: they were to remain there until two years later, when the 'Pilot's Dome' in Harmani, in the centre of the town, was ready as their new accommodation.[4]

Considering the high level of secrecy of the entire Objekt, it was more than a little surprising that just before the Czechoslovak crisis a Soviet military delegation, headed by aviation Marshall Vershinyin, visited Bihać AB! Indeed, the Yugoslavs even organised a demonstration of the full use of the underground facilities and a flying programme was run by one of the jets from the Batajnica-based 204th Fighter Regiment.[5] This visit not only confirmed that since Soviet weaponry began to flow into the country in 1961, and all the way up until the Warsaw Pact's aggression against Czechoslovakia, Tito's army had firmly regarded the Soviets as 'allies'; but high-ranking Soviet officers thus received the opportunity to not only tour the base, but to witness the way it was used before most of the RV i PVO could do so.

The 117th Fighter Regiment arrived at Bihać AB in late May 1968. Two of the R-13-armed MiG-21F-13 (L-12) are shown here being towed to an exit from Objekt Klek. (HDA)

At the peak of the crisis in Czechoslovakia, the 117th Regiment was actually still acclimatising itself to its new home-base. Nevertheless, the unit kept four aircraft on quick reaction alert (QRA) readiness 1, and another four on QRA readiness 2. All of its other jets were kept at readiness 3. The tempo of operations was also high and the unit lost two pilots during this period: one during a ferry sortie from Batajnica to Banja Luka, when a two-seat MiG-21U crashed, and another when a MiG-21F-13 crashed during an alert-take-off. Despite these tragic mishaps, later on the JRV i PVO concluded that the acclimatisation process of the 117th Regiment in its new base was 'very successful'.[6]

During the Czechoslovak Crisis in late summer 1968, the 117th Regiment maintained a four ship detachment at QRA or "Readiness No. 1". (Suad Hamzić)

That said, Bihać AB should have become operational back in 1965 and was lagging behind the schedule even as of August 1968. Thus, when the crisis caused the air force to move the 117th Regiment to its new home-base, the unit found itself lacking ground personnel in particular. Indeed, all the time until 1969, officers, NCOs and other ranks needed to work up to 16 hours a day to fully deploy and work-up their new and fascinating facilities. Throughout this time, the conditions on the base remained austere, as many of the installations outside the Objekt still had to be completed, and there was also much work to do inside the galleries. For example, the air conditioning did not work, and the humidity inside was oppressive. Another massive problem became the dust. The walls were sprayed with liquid cement: when this was dry, it tended to create immense amounts of dust that whenever there was intensive movement inside, for example, when a tractor would pass by, would rise not only into a cloud, but create a haze in the galleries. The problem was debated, extensively, in the course of multiple meetings of the members of the KPJ at the base. When no other solution was found, the decision was taken to paint all the walls within the Objekt in light blue. This finally solved the problem. 'The Party did it!', concluded the former pilot Ranko Kovačević.[7]

That said, this remained only one issue: there was no solution for many other problems. For example, the ventilation was constantly

Combat readiness No. 1 in Yugoslav practice included the pilot sitting in the cockpit, the aircraft fully-armed and connected to the APU, as seen here in September 1968. (S. Hamzić)

The winter of 1968-69 in Bihać was harsh. Here the "Rolba" is clearing the taxiways while pilots dressed in VKK-4 high altitude equipment with GSh-4M helmets prepare for flying. (Hajrudin Kolonić)

Lined up ground crew of the 117th Regiment await Tito's inspection. The MiGs are attached to electric tractors. (MJ)

noisy, while artificial lights and humidity made any work inside the Objekt very hard to endure. Before long, the personnel began spending only the minimum time necessary inside, while the rest of the work was undertaken on the aprons, in the huts outside the Klek, or on improvised sport fields nearby.

Marshal Tito's Visit

As the Objekt was finally completed, on 3 May 1969, Marshal Tito paid his first visit to the facility, together with the top brass of the socialist republics of Croatia and Bosnia and Herzegovina. The visit took almost a day, and began with the inspection of lined-up personnel of the 200th Air Base and the 117th Regiment, before the visitors toured the Objekt to see the galleries, technical centre, classrooms, and then engage in small-talk with pilots and ground crew. Then, the President of the SFRJ and the Commander-in-Chief of the Yugoslav Armed Forces was taken to the open terrace of the air traffic control to observe an exercise in which several units of the RV i PVO took part: these included SOKO Kraguj COIN fighters from Cerklje AB, SOKO G-2 Galebs, and six MiG-21s from the 117th Fighter Regiment. Finally, a luncheon was organised for Tito and the airmen from the Bihać units and other pilots involved in the exercise. At the end of his visit, the Yugoslav strongman signed the Visitor's Book, leaving behind positive remarks on the units and the base.[8]

Tito's visit was overshadowed by the crash-landing of Lieutenant Sluganović of No. 125 Squadron in his MiG-21F-13. During the landing, one of the main landing gear legs would not extend and the MiG swung off the runway, its ejection seat fired automatically and launched the pilot out of the cockpit. Young Sluganović hit the ground at the edge of the runway.[9] He was collected in a

Fiat Campagnola and rushed to Bihać hospital where he died an hour later, while Tito was still in luncheon. The commander of the regiment informed the commander of the RV i PVO about Sluganović's accident. The news was grim and Tito offered to have the pilot taken to his personal aircraft to be ferried to a military hospital in Belgrade, but the Air Force top brass said that the pilot was already in Bihać hospital and was conscious.[10] Thus, Tito was spared from bad news: obviously, the generals thought it would have been a disaster that his first visit to the air base and underground Objekt should be marked with such a tragic event.

In 1970, Marshal Tito visited Bihać air base again. He was host to the Sudanese president General Jaffar an-Nimeiry. The two arrived onboard Tito's Ilyushin Il-18 and were welcomed by the top brass of the RV i PVO. Inside the base, the hosts were the new commander of the 117th Regiment, Lieutenant-Colonel Ristić and commander of No. 125 Squadron Major Djilas. Tito and Nimeiry toured the whole underground Objekt and, after Nimeiry left, Tito waited for his spouse, Jovanka, to arrive on board a Sud Aviation SE.210 Caravelle airliner, slightly late.[11]

Becoming Accustomed to the Objekt

The winter with its snow and sharp winds was another problem which was discovered when the air base became operational. To keep the flying and training on schedule, the 117th Regiment moved to Zemunik AB, next to Zadar, on the coast of the Adriatic Sea: this re-deployment took place whenever necessitated by the meteorological situation in the Bihać area.

By the beginning of the 1970s, the galleries in the Objekt were still not fully operational for the complete pre-flight preparation of the MiGs. Systems for aircraft refuelling and signaling were still incomplete; the pipelines for high pressure oxygen (250At) were not yet installed, and there were none of the installations necessary

On 3 May 1969 Tito accompanied by his wife and Federal, Bosnian, and Croatian politicians, and top military commanders of the JNA, paid a visit to Bihać Air Base. Visible above is the KPJ's inscription, 'Your life and combat readiness of the unit depend on strict respect of rules'.

Tito, accompanied by military, political, and party top brass, and his wife Jovanka, being shown how the Technical Centre of Objekt Klek works. (MJ)

Tito shakes hands with the pilots of No. 125 Fighter Squadron under the watchful eyes of the RV I PVO commander General Bubanj, No. 125 Squadron CO Major Djilas, and the 117th Regiment commander Lt Colonel Zlatić. (MJ)

Tito receives a model of MiG-21F-13 from the airmen of the 117th Fighter Regiment. (MJ)

During Tito's visit, No. 460 Light Combat Aviation Squadron from Cerklje arrived to demonstrate the combat capabilities of its brand new light piston-engined Soko Kraguj aircraft. Deployment of other units to Bihać was very rare and for large events and exercises only. (MJ)

Tito and Nimeiry were driven through the underground Objekt. Here they pass the entrance of the Air Technical Workshop, the entrance of which was adored with extensive quotes of Tito. (MJ)

A line of MiG-21F-13s of No. 352 Squadron in Gallery D, Objekt Klek, 1969. (HDA)

The same gallery in 1970: now featuring brand new reconnaissance MiG-21Rs (L-14i) with the inevitable Bulgarian electric tug-tractors. (HDA)

Another visit from Tito was organised in 1970, when he accompanied Sudanese president General Jaafar Nimeiry. At that time the 117th Regiment had converted to MiG-21PFM (L-14), an example of which, No. 22708, can be seen here fully armed. (MJ)

for the work of the photo-section and the section responsible for reconnaissance pods for No. 352 Squadron: indeed, surplus armament was kept in temporary storage in the emptied village of Baljevac, inside houses bought from the locals.[12] Finally, regardless what kind of instructions for the use of the Objekt had been issued in 1968, first-hand experience tended to result in the re-writing of many of these.

One of the principal issues was the strict regime of movement inside the Objekt, which dictated daily life. Suad Hamzić explained:

> The regime of activities and moving in the underground Objekt was strictly regulated [based] upon the working task and level of authority of the particular airmen. It was controlled by the military police. We had special passes for entry to the underground Objekt and moving inside of it. Colour and highly visible stripes on the passes enabled the person to enter certain premises or installations. Even when I was the Deputy Commander of No. 352 Squadron and had received a pass with a red diagonal stripe – which granted me an unlimited

access – I never entered and thus never knew the looks of, for example, the ammunition depots; nor that of the fuel storage with hundreds of tons of kerosene... and other similar materials in reserve.[13]

Lining up of the 117th Regiment personnel outside entrance No. 2, 1970. In the rear, two liaison/training Aero-3a and an F-86E Sabre act as some kind of gate-guardian. (Ilija Zlatić family)

In his memoirs, Hamzić continued, describing the Objekt as:

> ... Indestructible and even invulnerable with the contemporary ordnance available to possible aggressors. The profile of galleries, their walls and blast deflectors, heavy automatic armoured doors... all looked impressive and impregnable. But it was obvious that the Objekt would have been vulnerable to demolition raids, sabotages in the vicinity of the aircraft, flammable materials and installations... That is the reason why the Objekt was heavily guarded by multiple watches, ambushes, patrols with dogs, fences and technical devices.[14]

Some of the intrusions of the foreign diplomats were noted in 1969-1971, but apparently less than in the period when the base was still under construction: for example, one forced landing of a foreign light aircraft was noted in this period. The HQ of the V Air Corps concluded that the foreign intelligence services '... used all the possible means to collect facts' on the unique air base. Military security also noted that part of the constructional documentation of the Objekt Klek was lost in 1969! While no further details were ever recorded, the conclusion was that this caused 'severe damage to the security'. The base was compromised again in 1970: not only through the visit of the Sudanese president, but also through visits of civilian journalists working for daily newspapers in Belgrade, Sarajevo, Zagreb, and Ljubljana, and the journalists of the Radio-Television Zagreb. Moreover, a worker of the civilian enterprise Union Invest, involved in various 'finishing works' inside the Objekt, lost the drawings for the ventilation system inside the photo-section. The security service of the RV i PVO subsequently concluded that, 'taking everything into account, it is certain that the Objekt Klek was discovered, and that its location, purpose, and most of its interior are known...'[15]

117th Regiment's Activities

In the period after the Czechoslovak Crisis, the Regiment reached its initial operational capability (IOC) status. It could carry out interceptions with single or pair of aircraft with classical guidance from the ground, or in the 'free hunt', by daylight and in good visibility, and – partially – by night and good visibility, from altitudes of 1,000 to 14,000 metres. Additionally, No. 125 Squadron was capable of carrying out ground attack missions. Conversion to the MiG-21PFM (L-14 under the Yugoslav military nomenclature system), in 1970, further boosted the capabilities of the regiment, even if this process caused lots of hardship for all the involved personnel – who were badly overstretched pulling normal duties and standing the QRA while undergoing training – even more so once the third squadron, No. 352, entered the process of converting to the brand-new MiG-21Rs, leaving the interceptor duties to the other two units. The air base then experienced a major problem due to a major malfunction of the landing equipment, which limited it to operations by visual flight conditions only for an extended period of time. Moreover, Runway No. 2 had to be shut down for nearly eight

Two of the MiG-21PFMs being towed inside Objekt Klek at entrance No. 2, monitored by a military policeman, in 1970. (HDA)

Several of the MiG-21U (NL-12) two-seaters were deployed to Bihać during the conversion to the MiG-21PFM in 1969-1971. (via Borislav Pejic)

months: this prompted some testing of the auxiliary grass runway named Čičkov Gaj, during the same period: while MiG-21PFMs proved capable of operating from this, the practice was eventually abandoned. It was thus only around 1973 that the 117th Regiment could be considered a fully operational unit, consisting of Nos. 124 and 125 Squadrons tasked with air defence and ground attack, while No. 352 Squadron was still working itself up through training for aerial photo-reconnaissance with help of container R, and then electronic reconnaissance (ELINT) missions with help of container D (for details, see colour section).[16]

Early 1970s: Large Exercises

Flying and training at Bihać Air Base was further intensified during the early 1970s, when the RV i PVO became involved in a series of large-scale exercises. Probably the largest exercise ever held in the former Yugoslavia was Sloboda 71 (Freedom 71), run in the Lika and Kordun areas of Croatia from 2 until 9 October 1971. Following the manoeuvre plan, the 126th Fighter Squadron of the 204th Regiment moved from Batajnica to Bihać AB, while the complete 117th Regiment moved from Bihać to Pleso AB.[18] This is how the MiG-21Ms came to operate from Objekt Klek for the first time as this version was never used by the 117th Regiment. During the exercise the units used shortened exercise two-digit tittles: the "17" and "24" Regiment or "20" Air Base. During the manoeuvre, a fuel installation in the underground Objekt was tested reaching up to 120 fuellings in a single day.

Exercise Poskok 72 (Viper) held between 21 and 23 April 1972 included airborne landing at several air bases, including Bihać. Even more so, Bihać was targeted by heliborne landings and it was the first time that exercise included the ground defence of the air base.

At 04:00 on 22 April, the 200th Air Base was put on alert: all personnel took positions and prepared the defence of the base. As preparation for the paratrooper assault a flight of ageing Republic F-84G Thunderjets from the 82nd Aviation Brigade based at Cerklje, carried out an attack on Bihać Air Base. Flying in the "low-low" regime, they managed to reach Bihać Air Base without being noticed by the air surveillance radars and were only spotted by the visual observing station, which alerted the air base. Only five MiG-21PFMs managed to take-off to intercept the attackers.

At 08:00 there were airborne and helicopter landings by paratroopers of 63rd Parachute Brigade. After 48 minutes of "fighting", well trained paratroopers managed to capture the Triangle apron in front of the entrances to the Objekt and set explosives and "destroy" it. In the following part of the exercise, the 200th Air Base was given the chance to match the airborne troops and they were surrounded and "destroyed". In the analyses of the exercise it was marked that positive experiences in organising the "sector defence" of the air base was gathered. The paratroopers were criticised for showing "too much persistence".

No matter the absence of the further comment on the exercise, it was obvious that the aggressors managed to reach Bihać Air Base by flying low-level, unnoticed by the radars, and that the enemy paratroopers managed in less than an hour to reach the main entrance of the underground Objekt. We can presume that the pilots of the 117th Regiment and radar operators of the 5th Air Surveillance Regiment were later trained to carry out their intercepting missions much faster, but Bihać Air Base was never reinforced with any infantry or armoured assets and neither of the neighbouring garrisons facilitated the larger force for defence of the base. Most likely, it was considered that air base's situation deep in Yugoslav territory was sufficient and that there was no need for any reinforcement of its defence.

In September 1972, the 200th Air Base and 117th Fighter Regiment were engaged in a large exercise above the middle of the Adriatic Sea, named Podgora 72. Part of the air base moved to Mostar where they supported the activities of No. 352 Reconnaissance Squadron during the exercise.[19]

This tempo of exercises continued later in 1974 during the crises with Italy. In all of these cases the ground crews of the 200th Air Base and 117th Regiment were deployed together to other air bases such

Table 2: Number of Aircraft by type within 117th Regiment, 1968-1972

Aircraft Type	1968	1969	1970	1971	1972
L-12	26	26	8		
L-14		8	16	23	22
L-14i		7	8	12	12
NL-12	8		5	4	4
NL-14					2
Kurir & Utva 66	2			2	2

The number of pilots varied from 49 to 66.[17]

as Mostar (1972) and Ljubljana airport (1974).

In 1973, No. 352 Reconnaissance Squadron left the organisational structure of the 117th Regiment and became an independent squadron directly attached to the RV i PVO HQs until 1990. The squadron remained in the same facilities and continued to operate alongside the other two fighter squadrons of 117th Regiment.[20] The unit had improved the content of its own facilities: the photo laboratory, container section and intelligence room.

"Flying day" in 1971: a MiG-21PFM at the "triangle" during flight preparations. (Author's collection)

On the other hand, this period of Bihać Air Base's history was marked with several crash landings and incidents caused by the intensive training and conversions of 1969-1972. The exercises just added more stress and effort to the regular daily flying. The year of 1973 was the first year finished without accidents and loss of pilot life at Bihać Air Base. It was marked that the 117th Regiment "entered the stable and secure phase of training and all of the elements of life and work."[21]

Pilots of No. 352 Reconnaissance Squadron dressed in VKK-6 high altitude flying suits and with GSh-6 helmets, preparing for flying outside the Objekt. It was typical practice in the 1970s until some small huts were built later on for use by the pilots. (Marjan Matančić)

In this period, larger numbers of the younger air technical officers and NCOs were sent to serve in at Bihać in the air base or the regiment after finishing their academies. One of them, Rajko Lukić reveals the arrival of the group of 13 young sergeants from Rajlovac Air Technical School on 31 August 1973. After the arrival they received some additional wages and four free days to settle in the city. The conversion programme started immediately, based upon the specialities of each of the sergeants. After initial theoretical course in the Pilot's Dome in the city, they were dispatched to the units in the air base. In the first month they carried out mutual work with more senior colleagues (so called: *stažiranje*). After they became independent, those who were of the general aviation speciality took charge of a single MiG-21, as was the practice, and the NCO had one or two conscripts as assistants. The other NCOs were specialists on different systems such as avionics, radios, radars, and some of them were armourers. These were not charged with the responsibility for certain aircraft, and they operated in shifts on the available airframes prepared for another day's activity. Lukić remembers:

I was charged with [a] fighter, and later converted to maintenance of the two-seater, "Sparka". The work was serious and professional. Contemporary rules of the Air Technical Service requested that one cannot leave the air base/go home, and to remain with the aircraft with malfunctions or not prepared... Working hours for the next day were ordered at the end of the actual working day. It happened that the working day started at dawn, or at the beginning of the working hours, or in the afternoon and sometimes in the evening. It was all connected with training activities upon the plan of the flying and training. We could be dispatched to serve a seven day shift at the QRA...[22]

Preparation of MiG-21PFMs of No. 125 Fighter Squadron in Gallery A, 1975. (M. Mustapić/MC Odbrana)

Ground crew park MiG-21PFM No. 22708. The aircraft had already been overhauled by Zmaj air depot, recognisable from the small rhomboid sign on the fin and typical painting of the squadron numbers on the front of the fuselage. This particular airframe was lost in a fatal incident on 24 August 1976. (via Ranko Kovačević)

Arrival of MiG-21Bis

It was expected in 1976 that the 117th Regiment would convert to the MiG-21 M/MF type.[23] Instead, two years later two entirely new versions – MiG-21bis (L-17) and MiG-21UM (NL-16) – were introduced to service. The initial conversion was carried out with the complete No. 124 Squadron and regimental HQ, and followed in 1979 by No. 125 Squadron at Batajnica AB: the process was continued and then completed back in Bihać. The surviving MiG-21PFMs were sent to Batajnica, leaving a few of them for flying proficiency with the regiment and No. 352 Squadron. 1978 was a difficult year concerning the weather conditions over the wider area, with frequent weather changes causing difficulties in carrying out the conversion in the new type. The year 1979 brought further improvement as, once the ground crews became accustomed to the new sub-variant, flying and further conversion of the personnel to the L-17 could be intensified. Indeed, most pilots quickly exceeded the planned 80 flying hours annually: most flew about 90, while some of more experienced fliers completed between 100 and 130. This was not just the sign of the improved flying activities, but also a clear indication of improved status of the ground crew, the technical branch of the base, and the improved condition of its facilities.[24]

Indeed, during the second half of the 1970s, the maintenance in the regiment and the air base improved to a degree where 92-93% of all aircraft were fully mission capable on average in 1976, 90% in 1978, and 91.6% in 1979: this in turn meant that at any given time, only one or two of the 46 MiG-21s assigned to the two combat units and the reconnaissance unit of the regiment was unserviceable,

Line of MiG-21Bis and Bis-Ks (L-17, L-17K). This type started to enter the inventory of the 117th Regiment in 1978-1980 and was operated by both No. 124 and No. 125 Squadrons. (via B. Pejić)

MiG-21Bis No. 17111 at the head of the line of No. 124 Squadron airframes in Gallery C. This aircraft was lost in a non-fatal crash on 9 September 1987. (Nikola Maravić family)

while all others were ready to be flown in combat operations at short notice.[25]

Table 3: MiG-21s of the 117th Regiment, 1977-1980

	MiG-21PFM (L-14)	MiG-21Bis (L-17)	MiG-21U (NL-12)	MiG-21UM (NL-16)
1977	21-24	-	2	-
1978	16	11 increased to 12	2	2
1979	16	12 increased to 15	2	2 increased to 4
1980	-	28	3	4

VIP Visitors

It seems that the commercial interests of Yugoslav military industry and foreign policy prevailed over the intentions to keep the underground air base in secrecy. The ambitions of the Yugoslav People's Defence Ministry were to sell the pattern of the base to any potential customer – especially diverse non-aligned allies in the so-called Third World. Correspondingly, after Numairy's visit of 1970, the next VIPs to visit Bihać AB were members of an Algerian military delegation in 1972.[26] Two years later, it was the Kuwait Air Force delegation that toured the Objekt. The Iraqis showed interest, too, and in September 1978 defence minister Colonel General Adnan Khairallah Talfah, with his two assistants, visited the base. The following month, Bihać was toured by the commander of the Iraqi Air Force with his assistants.[27] Finally, in September 1983 commander of the Indian Air Force, Air Chief Marshal Dilbag Singh with assistants, visited Bihać Air Base.[28]

Eventually, such visits 'did their job' and during the 1980s the Yugoslav defence sector was contracted at least by the Iraqis and the Kuwaitis to construct multiple air bases for them. The most famous amongst these was Project 202, which resulted in the construction of five major air bases, and an expansion and hardening of a similar number of facilities in Iraq, and the biggest of these was Project 202C, named al-Bakr AB (better known in the West as 'Balad'). The Iraqi contract was followed by one with Kuwait, which resulted in the construction of Ahmad al-Jaber (also known as 'Ahmadi' to the involved Yugoslavs) and Ali as-Salem Sabah ABs. Finally, the Angolans

Commander of the 117th Regiment Zijo Varešanović, and his chief of staff and later CO of the regiment Vladeta Kostić, walk back to the Objekt after a sortie. Behind can be seen a line of MiG-21Bis which briefly served at Bihać during 1980 and were transferred to Priština air base to equip 83rd Fighter Regiment there. (Vladeta Kostić family)

contracted the Yugoslavs to construct for them the Yuri Gagarin AB outside Namibe.

Teams of the Communist Party of Yugoslavia followed later in the 1970s. On the Air Force Day, on 19 and 21 May 1976, three delegations followed in quick succession, including one with the highest party and political representatives of Bosnia and Herzegovina on 19 May, Croatia on 21 May, and then the delegation of the Political Department of the Yugoslav Federal Ministry of Defence, headed by the assistant minister – and General of the JNA – Petkovski on 26-27 May. All of these delegations received the opportunity to tour the underground Objekt, and General Petkovski interviewed many of the pilots and ground crews, showing particular interest in their morale, political situation, and living conditions.[29]

In June 1978 and July 1980, participants of the highest Yugoslav military school, The School of the National Defence, visited the base as the part of their curriculum. In the 1980s the regime of the visits to the air base became more flexible and open. The air base was visited by the local authorities from the city of Bihać, then different institutions and schools from the city. They were followed by the participants of the School of the National Defence, then the cadets of the finishing years of the Military Air Technical Academy, members of the VII Army HQ from Sarajevo and many others, including the veterans of the 117th Regiment on 15 December every year up to 1991.[30]

Death of Marshal Tito

During the late 1970s, and because of the lasting illness of Marshal Tito, the Yugoslav armed forces were kept at higher combat readiness. It was expected that when he died, a 'possible foreign invader' may suddenly launch an aggression against Yugoslavia. This estimation drew no difference between NATO and the Warsaw Pact. Air defence systems were kept in high readiness, including the MiGs at Batajnica and Bihać. Marshal Tito's illness characterised the whole first half of 1980. When he died on 4 May of the same year, combat readiness reached its peak.

The fear of a possible invasion from both the NATO and the Warsaw Pact reached such proportions that during Tito's illness all of the units at Bihać Air Base were kept at permanent higher readiness status: one quarter of the personnel had to be present at any time of the day, and their working hours were extended from 06:00 to 18:00. When night flying was undertaken, pilots and ground crews worked for 16 hours. Officers assigned to the intelligence centre were constantly gathering information about the activity in neighbouring airspaces, while ground personnel deployed various obstacles in between the runways, so as to be able to quickly re-position them and thus block the air base in the case of a sudden airborne landing.

Eventually, the HQ of the 117th Regiment and the 51st Aerial Surveillance Battalion established a joint command post – the Group for Combat Command (GBK) – which operated 24/7, in two daily shifts, within the confined spaces of the underground Objekt. Simultaneously, No. 125 Squadron not only continued, but also

Douglas C-47s of the Pleso-based 111th Transport Regiment were frequent visitors to Bihać air base until the last few were replaced by Antonov An-26s in 1976-77. Here a group of pilots of No. 352 Squadron prepare to take off for an exercise at Slatina AB, outside Priština, in the then autonomous province of Kosovo i Metohija in southern Serbia. (Novica Šušić)

An unusual guest at Bihać was the Antonov AN-12, the largest RV i PVO transport plane. Young Sergeant Popović of No. 352 Squadron took the opportunity to pose in front of it. (Mirko Popović)

completed the conversion of its crews to the MiG-21bis' and MiG-21UMs – and this despite the lack of suitable manuals and other instructional literature in Serbo-Croat language. Instead, technical officers and the NCOs of the regiment took care to, in whatever was left of their 'off' time, translate whatever manuals they could get. During this period of extremely hard work, and regardless of all the hardships experienced by everybody involved, no wrongdoings were recorded by even one officer or other rank, and not one disciplinary measure had to be taken. On the contrary, 1980 went down in the history of the 117th Regiment as one with the highest average number of flying hours per pilot, a record-breaking fully mission capable rate of 92.5% for its MiG-21 fleet, and was concluded with both of its units converting to the new versions of the type.[31]

Improving Capabilities

The introduction to service of the more potent MiG-21bis enabled the 117th Regiment to vastly expand its overall capabilities. This variant came not only with its original, Soviet-made weapons – like advanced R-13M (ASCC/NATO-codename 'AA-2c Atoll') air-to-air missiles, but also with FAB-250M62 and FAB-500M62 bombs, the PLAB bomb series, launchers for 128mm unguided rockets, 240mm S-24 unguided rockets, and the British-made Hunting BL.755 cluster bomb units (CBUs). Correspondingly, during the early 1980s the unit became involved in a wide variety of exercises, and began regularly flying ground attack sorties. Indeed, by 1985, its primary task shifted from interception to strike.[32]

The other peculiarity was the wide range of annual deployments to other air bases, where the Bihać MiGs took part in the exercises, live firing or simply training in operations from different air bases in the area of responsibility of V Air Corps. Usually, the MiG-21bis flight or squadron would be followed by an An-26 transport with ground crew, who would take over maintenance at the air base where they had landed.

In order to improve maintenance, the Air Technical Company was taken out of the 200th Air Base and on 20 January 1984 transferred into the 117th Regiment, which up to then had an air technical platoon. The company was tasked with 2nd level of the air technical maintenance.

The MiG-21Bis-Ks (L-17Ks) were introduced to the 117th Regiment's inventory in July 1981. Here, 17212 taxies out. This particular aircraft was shot down by Croatian forces on 18 September 1991 with pilot Nuspahić onboard. (via B. Pejić)

Engine trials outside the Objekt on MiG-21Bis serialed 17128 in the beginning of the 1980s. The aircraft was lost in a crash on 16 August 1984. (Author's collection)

A significant boost in 1983 for No. 352 Reconnaissance Squadron was the introduction of the Fairchild-built aerial photo-reconnaissance camera KA-112A Long Range Aerial Panoramic Photographic system, or simply LORAP. On 1 August 1984, a photo-laboratory was set up in the underground facility in Bihać and the system became operational. A total of four MiG-21MFs (marked as L-15M) were converted to carry LORAP containers. The veteran MiG-21Rs continued to be used as platforms for Soviet reconnaissance pods. This system was an important step for the unit and another new type introduced into the premises of the Objekt.

In 1984, this squadron operated a variety of the MiG-21 types: nine Rs, five PFMs, four MFs, two UMs and a single liaison Utva 66, and the unit carried out a number of aerial reconnaissance sorties operating from other MiG-bases around Yugoslavia.[33]

The statistics from the second half of the 1980s showed that most of the scheduled and planned flying was carried out – the average percentage of flying was between 86 and 93 percent. The missing percentage was largely due to a lower rate within the night and IFR sorties, which

A line of freshly delivered MiG-21Bis of No. 124 Fighter Squadron during preparations for a flight, early 1980. (Author's collection)

Preparation of the MiG-21Bis-K No. 17202 on the apron at the beginning of the 1980s. (Author's collection)

Line-up of the 117th Regiment's MiGs in the mid-1980s. Right to left are examples of the MiG-21Bis and several MiG-21UMs (NL-16 and single NL-14) on the apron in front of Objekt Klek. (via B. Pejić)

Preparation of the MiG-21bis-K serial nubmer 17202 on the apron, in the early 1980s. (Authors' Collection)

were usually not carried up to the complete planned figures, contrary to regular daily and VFR sorties.[34]

Looking the documents of the 117th Regiment there were 109 planned flying days in 1989. In that year 83 flying days were completed, and 26 days partly. The average flying day included 52 taking-offs/sorties with an average time of 39 minutcs. Due to good weather and a higher number of non-planned assigned tasks and missions, the regiment logged 113 percent of planned sorties and 110 percent of flying hours, reaching almost average 78 hours per pilot.[35]

In the second half of the 1980s, the number of the qualified technicians was still only at around 83 percent of what was necessary and authorised. The Regimental HQ pointed out that the lack of technicians caused the decline in airworthiness to 85 percent, reducing the number of daily sorties from an average 61 in 1986 to an average 53 in 1987. This issue was addressed through the introduction of 'contract NCOs': technicians recruited from conscripts that had served their national service at Bihać, or civilians that joined the military and then underwent a short conversion course.

Another problem which influenced the regular operations was the overhauling and repairs of the Tumansky engines (so-called "MM"). The problem was particularly severe with the older versions of two-seat conversion trainers, like MiG-21U-400 and MiG-21U-600. During this period, the workshop at Bihać AB carried out between 18 to 21 non-planned engine replacements every year, all caused by different malfunctions.

In the last peacetime year of 1990, the squadrons in Bihać maintained a fully mission capable rate of between 71 percent and 88 percent every month, eventually reaching 81-84 percent over the year. There was a regular flow of the MiGs to and from overhauls at the

Table 4: Operational Status of No. 352 Squadron's MiG-21s, 30 October 1986				
	MiG-21Bis	MiG-21PFM	MiG-21UM	MiG-21US/early UM
operational/available	18/21	1/2	2/3	1/2

Ground crew of No. 352 Squadron parks a MiG-21R (26111) after the sortie. An underbelly "R" ELINT pod is visible. This airframe was claimed by the Croatian forces on 11 April 1992 over Kupres and pilot Grandić was captured after ejection. (Miloš Vukojčić)

MiG-21R of No. 352 Squadron equipped with a D day-light photo-reconnaissance pod, seen in Gallery D, mid-1980s. No. 26103 in front served until 2003 and it is now part of the Yugoslav Ari force museum. (Rade Djurić)

A group of No. 352 Reconnaissance Squadron pilots, headed by CO Major Stevo Janjanin (fifth from the left) observe flying in early 1983. In front of them a motley group of the MiGs belonging to the squadron: from left to right: 26107 (MiG-21R), 22951 (MiG-21UM), 22707 (MiG-21PFM), 26109 (MiG-21R), 22807 MiG-21M) and one unrecognisable. Interestingly, Janjanin had a crash landing in 22807 on 4 May 1983 and was shot down on 8 November 1991 and captured by Croatian forces while flying 26109! (Stevo Janjanin)

Zmaj Works. Local technicians finally managed to improve the maintenance to a degree where the number of non-planned engine replacements was reduced and, finally, seven MiG-21bis were acquired from the Batajnica AB, when No. 128 Squadron was disbanded.[36]

Overall, after the initial period 1968-1972, and up to the war of 1991, flying from Bihać was relatively safe. There were two fatalities in No. 352 Squadron (in 1975 and 1986), while in 117th Regiment there was one fatality in 1989 with loss of two pilots in a two-seater that crashed: the latter accident happened after 13 years of service without fatal incidents in this unit: a remarkable result by all measures, especially knowing the intensity of flying and difficulties with the runways at Bihać AB.

51st Air Surveillance Battalion

In the second part of the 1970s, Plješevica Mountain that overlook the air base was "discovered" as the possible site for the location of an advanced long-range, early warning radar, and the works began almost instantly at the peak called Gola Plješevica. This radar site was completed in 1978, and the first radar system deployed. While definitely an excellent position, operating this radar station proved a major problem: just the provision of such basic necessities as food and water was a complex issue, even more so during the winter, when the mountain was completely covered in snow, and the only road leading to the peak was blocked.

To operate this station, 51st Aerial Surveillance Battalion was established in 1978, including its HQ and the 1st Company. The latter consisted of two platoons, including the HQ Squad (Četa za komandovanje, ČZK), equipped with Soviet-made P-35, PRV-11, and P-12 radars, and protected by three Yugoslav-made 20mm

Table 5: MiG-21s of the 117th Regiment, 31 October 1990

	MiG-21Bis	MiG-21R	MiG-21MF	MiG-21 PFM	MiG-21 US/UM	MiG-21U
31 October 1990	31	10	4	3	3	2

M55 20/3 three-barrel anti-aircraft guns. Its second element was equipped with a British-made Marconi S-654 radar, supported by a S-5014B Furnus cabin. At the time, this combination was considered one of the most advanced systems of its kind in the world: with its confirmed detection range of more than 400 kilometres, it was capable of tracking not only all the aerial movements over western Yugoslavia, but also most of the Adriatic Sea, much of northern Italy, all of southern and eastern Austria, and most of the Hungarian airspace.

Both elements came into being in the Željava barracks, right next to the HQ of 200th Air Base; the Operations Centre (OC) of 51st Aerial Surveillance Battalion came into being at the underground objekt coded as k.377 (constructed in 1977 inside the Abdića Brdo). Once operational, the OC and the ČZK were deployed atop of the same hill: with this, and for the first time ever, the MiGs from Bihać could be supported by ground control for the duration of their entire sortie. The second platoon was deployed at Gola Plješevica, at the k.1648/1650, about 25 kilometres from Bihać: its equipment was calibrated in June 1979 and – initially linked to the OC and the ČZK by the Vozdukh-1P of Soviet origin (named Vazduh in RV i PVO) automatic tactical management system (ATMS) – declared operational on 29 November of the same year. Operational 24 hours a day, whenever in need of maintenance, this crucial installation was replaced by the radars at k.377.[37]

In May 1984, the OC of 51st Aerial Surveillance Battalion was re-located from k.377 to the Objekt at Bihać AB. Simultaneously, the obsolete and much too complex Vozdukh-1P was replaced by the new ATMS of British origin used to link-up all the elements of the battalion, designated AS-74, while the radar system was replaced by the British-made Marconi S-600 radar.[38] The AS-74, with the Furnus cabin, was to remain operational until September 1991, while the OC of the 51st Aerial Surveillance Battalion served as the joint command post for both that unit and the 117th Regiment – at both Objekt Klek and the k.377.[39] Moreover, its introduction to service prompted a reorganisation of the ČZK: henceforth, guidance duties were taken over by the OC of the 51st Aerial Surveillance Battalion.

In 1984 a CD-2 radar for civil air traffic control was also positioned on Gola Plješevica, by when the S-600 radar was covered by an M68 arctic dome made by ECKO, a British company from Stratford. Moreover, the isolated crews atop the hills were stocked with food and received their own diesel generators (each station also had a spare) to generate electrical power. Finally, each position received two US-made 12.7mm Browning M2 machine guns for defence purposes.[40]

The first overhaul of the S-600 at Plješevica – and the first work of this kind undertaken by the RV i PVO – was carried out the maintenance company of the 5th Regiment and Kosmos Air Depot in 1985.Two years later, the 51st Aerial Surveillance Battalion was reinforced through the addition of the US-made Westinghouse AN/TPS-70 three-dimensional (3D) radar, positioned atop Abdića Brdo. It became the core of the independent light movable radar station of the unit. The final upgrade of the equipment of this unit concerned the replacement of the AS-74 ATMS by the more modern AS-84 in 1991.[41]

Overall, during the second half of the 1980s, the air control segment of Bihać AB – 51st Aerial Surveillance Battalion – was composed as follows:

51st Centre and Command Company for Objekt Klek and Željava barracks, with joint OC in the Objekt and a reserve at the Abdića Brdo;

- 1st Company, including:
    - 1st Platoon at Abdića Brdo (equipped with the P-35, PRV-11, four power generators, four anti-aircraft guns, and support vehicles), and

Inside the cab of the Vozdukh-1P ATMS: this served the purpose of integrating the information gathered from different radar sites and providing their combined radar picture to the air defence HQ. The Vozdukh-1P (and, later on, the AS-74) was capable of integrating the work of aerial surveillance systems, manned interceptors, and units operating surface-to-air missiles, and enabled the HQ to simultaneously control operations against up to 48 targets. (HDA)

P-35 (left) and PRV-11 (right) radars at the Abdića Brdo/k.377. This position had a small underground facility for command purposes which is visible in the foreground. (HDA)

Known as "SAVAKS" (derived from initial letter S and AWACS), Sergeant Savo Rajić, was regarded among pilots of Bihać AB as the best as most reliable radar guidance officer. (B.Pejic)

The men of the 51st Air Surveillance Battalion work on the Abdića Brdo position in the late 1980s. (via Rajica Bošković)

Two sergeants of 51st Battalion: Pavić and Vefić, near the newly acquired US-made Westinghouse AN/TPS-70, one of the most advanced 3D-radars in the 1970s, atop k.377 (Abdića Brdo) in 1987-1988. (via R. Bošković)

- 2nd Platoon at Gola Plješevica (equipped with the S-654, S-605 and S-605S, associated support cabins, S-5014B operational cab, S-613 height-finder, CD-2 "secondary" civil radar linked to main surveillance radar, generators AD 180 and AD10, and two AAA Browning machine guns),
- 1st Independent (mobile) Radar Platoon, deployed at the Abdića Brdo (equipped with the US-made AN/TPS-70).
- Communications Company, deployed in Čelopek. [42]

According to the contemporary commander of 1st Company, Captain Mirsad Gadžun, guidance of the MiG fighters was carried out from the CP at Plješevica – in both classic (voice-over-radio) or automatic way (the later consisted of steering MiGs via remote control), and from Abdića Brdo in semi-automatic and later the classic way only.[43]

200th Air Base in the 1980s

Throughout the whole period of its existence, the 200th Air Base headquarters remained located outside Objekt Klek and was situated in the village of Željava. Near the base, was the HQ of 200th Light Air Defence Artillery Regiment, the largest unit of the air base. In the same Objekt were the HQs of the other two units that were in the complex of the air base: 51st Air Surveillance Battalion and 379th Engineer Battalion. The 51st Air Surveillance Battalion was part of the 5th Air Surveillance Regiment, while 379th Engineer Battalion directly reported to V Air Corps. Both of those HQs were located in Zagreb.

During the 1970s, 379th Engineer Battalion and Engineer Company of 200th Air Base continued to work on the facilities outside of the Objekt. They built positions for AA artillery, storage, other facilities and carried out forestation to mask the Objekt from the air. In 1971, 200th Air Base built four hardened bunkers and the operations centre at Čelopek. The engineer unit of the Fifth Army built 22 machinegun bunkers in 1972-73.[44]

In an attempt to improve the conditions in Bihać Air Base, several novelties were introduced: a new NCOs dome, a mobile canteen to supply the personnel on the aprons and around the air base, finishing the traffic control outside the Objekt, and building the fortifications at Vedro Polje and Vaganac.[45] In 1985, the road between the Objekt and village of Željava was covered with asphalt; there were works on power cables and the road to the radar position at Gola Plješevica.

Slowly, the members of the units became accustomed to the base's conditions and the improvements. The walls were painted, air conditioning was improved and the floors were covered with plastic floor-cloth. In 1978, a new classroom and intelligence operational room was created. The classroom link-trainer TL-14 *Комплексный тренажер самолета КТС-4М* (Integrated Flight Simulator) for the MiG-21 was also introduced.

In the early days of the air base's existence communication between the facilities was difficult. If there were no vehicles available personnel would have to walk. Later, and especially in the 1980s, a shuttle coach was introduced cruising the air base, with starting point at air base HQ and departing at every hour during working hours.

The 200th Air Base CO had a permanent telephone/radio link with each of the commanders around the air base. Every week an official conference was held with the commanders of the 117th Regiment and No. 352 Squadron. With the commanders of the 51st Air Surveillance and 379th Engineer Battalion there were monthly conferences.

Complications of Yugoslavia's inner politics, and large scale protests in Kosovo, led to a visit by the federal minister of Defence, Army General Nikola Kadijević to Bihać AB, from 22 to 24 February 1989. The general toured the Objekt, conferred with the commanders of the units at the base, and finished his visit with a speech in which he stressed the 'preservation of the unity' of the JNA and the JRV i PVO to the gathered personnel. A few days later, on 26 October, the air base was visited by Dragutin Zelenović, member of the Yugoslav Presidency, who also toured the underground facilities and the radar site at Gola Plješevica, above the air base.

By the late 1980s and after the introduction to service of the MiG-29 at Batajnica AB, it was planned that in the foreseeable future, Bihać

General Kadijević, (second from right) accompanied by generals Mirčetić, Tus, Maravić and other assistants, monitors QRA reaction in the Operations Centre of Objekt Klek. (Milan Menićanin)

Member of the Yugoslav Presidency, Dragutin Zelenović (left) inspected Bihać Air Base on 26 October 1989. Here, he listens to the explanation of Major Grbović, in the parachute section inside the "Star", Objekt Klek. (Milinko Grbović family)

AB should also receive this type of fighter. However, the problem was that the entire Objekt was designed with the MiG-21 – or another fighter of similar dimensions – in mind. The MiG-29 had two vertical stabilisers and it was not possible to move it through the entry doors because of the massive 'concrete curtain', which only had a cut-out for a single-finned aircraft. Therefore, in 1990 works on expanding the Entry A began, to enable the towing of MiG-29s into the Objekt: however, the construction in question was abandoned in 1991.

3
Inside Bihać Air Base

Alongside Sombor, Bihać was the only garrison in Yugoslavia where the commanding officer came from the Air Force. The city of Bihać itself was the ground forces garrison, and the 200th Air Base commander had all garrison responsibilities. In the city there was the "27 July" barracks with the Quartermaster Training Battalion belonging to the Fifth Army (HQ in Zagreb) and several small HQs for the development of war-time infantry units. The "Grmeč" barracks were in the village of Žegar and there was storage in the villages of Ripač, Račić, Pokoj and as far as in Svodna near Prijedor. Besides those which were used by the Air Force, most of them kept armament for war-time army and Territorial Defence units of the Bihać, Cazin, Velika Kladuša, Bosanska Krupa, Bosanski Novi and Bosanski Petrovac communities. In addition there was a large estate at Harmani in the downtown of Bihać, where most of the airmen lived with their families. There was also the 5th Army range at Slunj.[1]

Garrison Bihać

The arrival of the air base and other RV i PVO units, actually improved the development of the city of Bihać. The estate of Harmani was built to accommodate the families of the military at the air base by the beginning of the 1970s. It continued to expand almost until the war in 1992. The policy of providing the young airmen with housing in order to adapt more easily to serving in Bihać was well established. Prior to the war building H-18 was settled with airmen and their families. The number of army apartments reached 1,000.

Local political structures highly valued this sudden boost to their city and remained friendly and most cooperative until the couple of months prior to arrival of the war in this area in spring 1992. Suddenly, numerous airmen arrived in this remote garrison leaving behind an established life in Zagreb or Belgrade. As Ranko Krivokapić, one of the pilots from initial groups remembers, the lifestyle in the new garrison did not resembled that at any other air base. Bihać was a true *casaba* with *asphalt od kina do benzina* (asphalt from cinema to petrol station) as he remembered. It was a local pedestrian street, "the corso", where locals gathered in the evenings that formed some kind of city centre.[2]

One of the top cadets (those who were the first in the generation were officially named "Tito's cadets") from the Air Academy in Zadar and Air Technical Academy in Rajlovac, Second Lieutenant Milan Tepšić recalls his arrival at Bihać Air Base in September 1985. Depending if they were pilots or technicians the newcomers were settled in the new or old Flyer's Dome in the city. Young newcomers were received by the "three most important men in the town": the city mayor and the commanders of the

Federal Minister of Defence General Veljko Kadijević (centre) inspected Bihać Air Base in February 1989. Here, inside Objekt Klek, led by Colonel Menićanin (far right), and followed by generals Tus, commander of the RV i PVO (right), and Mirčetić, CO of V Air Corps (left). (Milan Menićanin)

The CO of No. 124 Squadron Major Mežnar with his air-technical platoon CO Second Lt Tepsic, seen here in front of the MiG-21Bis-K line in 1985. (Milan Tepšić)

200th Air Base of the 117th Regiment. Tepšić remembered that the CO of the 117th Regiment finished his introduction speech by saying "Everybody knows that you have arrived. And now they see you, especially the girls!" It was true, the city's potential brides were cheerful with every new officer in the town. But the arrival of the new second lieutenants and sergeants was much more welcomed by the veterans of the regiment and air base. It meant that the same number of them would be allowed to leave Bihać and to transfer to some much more civilised air base or HQ in Belgrade or Zagreb. On the other side the process of leaving the "old bones" and the arrival of newcomers from academies and schools caused the regiment – and to some extent the air base – to have the youngest personnel in the air force, averaging around 27.5 years.[3]

Bihać air base would remain a garrison where most of the personnel tried to leave as soon as possible. In 1970, among 280 transfer requests in V Air Corps, there were 105 from Bihać Air Base, including 68 from 200th Air Base and 37 from 117th Regiment. The harsh living and working conditions led to a constant lack of active personnel. In 200th Air Base staffing was up to 92 percent for officers and NCOs, while in 117th Regiment it was less: 89 percent for NCOs, but 74.5 percent for officers! It was the lowest rate of manpower among the units of V Air Corps. 200th Air Base had a constant problem with reserve personnel throughout late 1960s and 1970s, since most of the local conscripts, after serving their mandatory service, emigrated to West Germany and other West European countries to work and live there.[4]

Improved living conditions came in the 1970s. The arrival of younger pilots and technicians, without wider professional experience or families, enabled stabilisation of the human resources policy at the air base. Some of the airmen, especially technicians and ground crew, started to marry the local girls and established families in the city.

Although not as serious as the late 1960s or early 1970s, the problem of personnel remained in the 1980s. Bihać did not improve its position on the list of prefered RV i PVO air bases and other than officers and NCOs fresh from academies, posting to a duty at this air base was still regarded as a kind of punishment. There were few air force personnel who requested Bihać for their service and in most cases they were those who were native to the area. It led to a situation where the flying units had only up to 70 percent of the needed technical personnel.

Structure of the 200th Air Base

In general 200th Air Base had a similar structure and tasks as any other air base in the Yugoslav Air Force – the exception was the underground Objekt. Since maintenance was organised in the Objekt, after the arrival of 117th Regiment in 1968, the reorganisation was carried out: its communications platoon and maintenance platoon were transferred to 200th Air Base. Each of the air technical platoons inside of the squadrons was enlarged and reorganised into air technical company.[5] On 20 January 1984, the Air-Technical Company for Maintenance was formed in the regiment, by taking out 30 technical personnel of 200th Air Base.[6]

According to documents from the beginning of the 1980s, 200th Air Base was defined as a "joint aviation unit tasked for the logistic and combat support of the two squadrons of the 117th Fighter Regiment and independent No. 352 Reconnaissance Squadron at the permanent air base of Bihać. [and] For the other squadrons of light jet combat or support aviation at the other airfields in the area of responsibility. This makes five squadrons in total."[7]

The area of responsibility of 200th Air Base covered the territory between the towns of Bosanska Gradiška, Bugojno, Bosansko Grahovo, Gospić, Delnice, Metlika and Glina. It spread over the territories of three Socialist Republics: Bosnia and Herzegovina, Croatia and partly Slovenia, now all independent states. It covered the aerodromes and divided these into three categories:

- A: Bihać AB,
- B: Udbina FOB (constructed as an air base but without active units permanently deployed), and
- C: Urije FOB, near Prijedor; Medeno Polje FOB, near Bosanski Petrovac; and Otočac FOB (these were grass airfields prepared to function as temporary bases for light jets or piston-powered combat aircraft).

The units that belonged to 200th Air Base were organised in five sections based upon their tasks and usage. The sections were not organised units, but were under various assistants to the air base commander's field of responsibilities:

- Combat and flying support section, headed by the chief of staff. It included: an infantry company, light air defence artillery regiment, communications company, NBC platoon, meteorological station and Pilot's Dormitory (in the town of Bihać);

During the existence of Bihać Air Base there were barracks at Željava where the units of the 200th Air Base, 379th Engineer and 51st Air Surveillance Battalions were located. Here, is seen one of the ceremonies of 200th Air Base (M. Menićanin)

- Rear support section, headed by the CO's assistant, including the automobile company, quartermaster platoon, fire-fighting platoon, ambulance and building section;
- Air technical and technical support section, with the CO's assistant as the head. It included: air technical and technical workshops, air technical support platoon, maintenance operations platoon and air technical and technical stores;
- Political section with the deputy commander; for political work including the soldiers' club at the air base and army club and garrison library in the city of Bihać;
- Security section with the CO's assistant for security issues with its section and military police platoon. The Security Section was in charge of all the security officers at all battalion sized units including the Engineer and Air Surveillance battalions, and the three squadrons of the fighter regiment. The air base had its military police unit tasked to take care of the air base issues as well for the other facilities and barracks and the city of Bihać itself.

Objekt Klek was a separate entity within 200th Air Base and its commander was directly subordinated to the air base commander (under the initial manual, dated May 1968, the commander of 200th Air Base was operationally subordinated to the CO Fighter Regiment). It was responsible for organising the work of all technical services to provide continuous operational and combat capability for the regiment, with supplying all necessary devices, armament and materials, fire-fighting, necessary means of protection, traffic organisation, feeding, and internal security. It was ranked as a battalion-sized unit, and it comprised of technicians of all branches, including technical, electric, building, and plumbing. They were tasked to maintain the Objekt from minor repairs to constant care of the air conditioning system and temperature.[8]

In the village of Željava, which was inside the base perimeter, were barracks consisting of 34 different buildings to house the conscript soldiers, vehicles, equipment, the workshops, and boiler rooms used by the units of 200th Air Base, as well as 379th Engineer Battalion and 51st Aerial Surveillance Battalion.

Under the organisational charts dated 8 January 1980, 200th Air Base had total of 1,027 personnel on peace-time strength, which would increase to 1,910 at war, while 379th Engineer Battalion had 343 personnel on strength (598 in case of war). The unit responsible for air defence of 200th Air Base was 200th Light Air Defence Artillery Regiment: this included 161 officers and other ranks, equipped – as of 2 April 1982 – with 32 M55 20/3 20mm, 6 Praga 30/2 30mm, and 6 Bofors L70/40 40mm anti-aircraft guns, and 10 Strela-1M (ASCC/NATO-codename 'SA-7 Grail') launchers. Not included in these numbers were the personnel of 117th Fighter Regiment (209 in peace and 354 at war), and the personnel of No. 352 Reconnaissance Squadron (147 in peace and 184 at war). Overall, the full complement of the air base was thus at around 2,000.[9]

Outside Bihać AB, there were the following storage depots:

- Aerial Armament Storage in the village of Bosanski Novi,
- Fuel Storage in the village of Pokoj, and
- Air Technical and Technical Storage in the village of Ripač.

As noted earlier, these stores existed before 200th Air Base was established. Later in 1989, the Quartermaster Storage in Bihać was integrated into 200th Air Base.[10]

Except for the aviation units, the Air Base resembled a USAF Wing in its responsibilities. The air technical maintenance provided the so-called II and III level of air maintenance for the aircraft of the regiment and reconnaissance squadron. One Yugoslav peculiarity in the structure of the air base was its political section. Another was that the security of the base was not perceived as the part of the mission support, but it was a separate entity with a direct link to the air base's CO. The chief of security was also in control of a parallel chain of command of the Security Service, where he reported not just to the CO of 200th Air Base, but also to the Chief of the Military Security of V Air Corps.

The last commanding officer of 200th Air Base, Colonel Milan Menićanin, described the base as 'a true nightmare to secure'. The total of ten guard posts were spread along and inside the perimeter, manned by about 160 officers and other ranks, and supported by 28 military dogs at any given time: this was the permanent duty of 200th Light AD Artillery Regiment and 200th Infantry Company. The dogs used for guarding were trained at a base constructed specially for this purpose in Pokoj: there, the dogs underwent special training – as usual within the JNA, where canines were always trained in special centres, depending on their task.[11]

Overall, commander of 200th Air Base was responsible for many other things than simply flying operations from the base. In peace

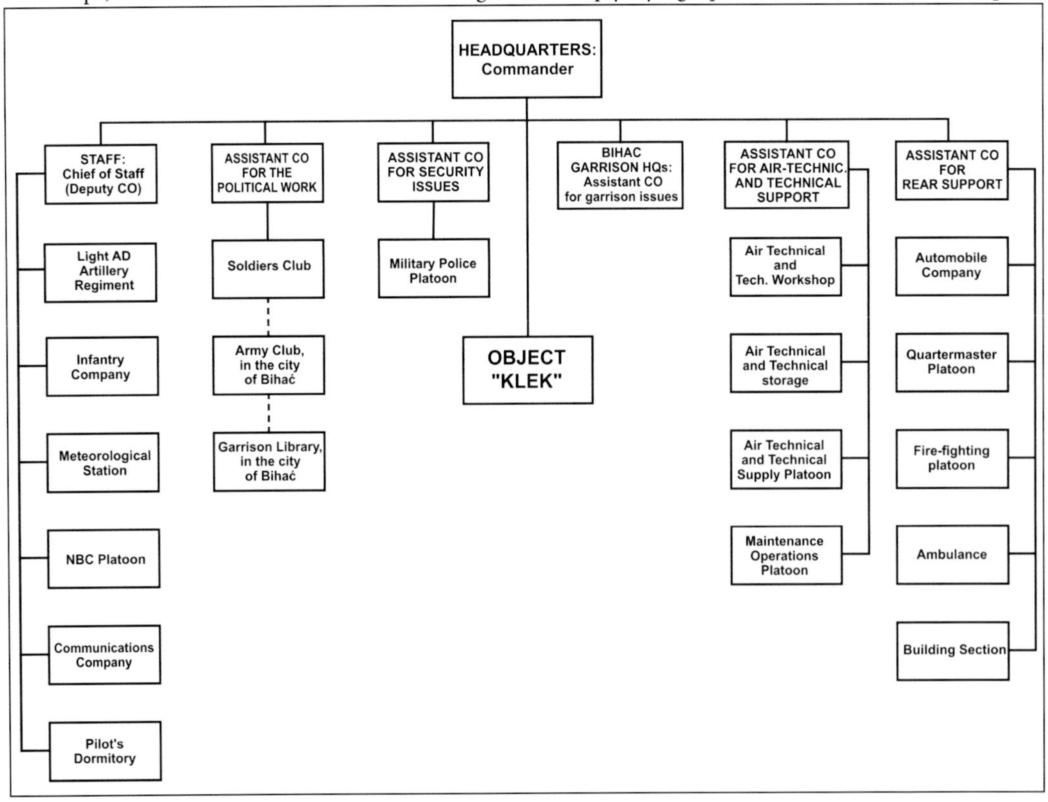

Organisational structure of 200th Air Base as of 1983. (Annual History of 117th Regiment)

Inspection of 200th Light Artillery AD Regiment in the mid-1980s: Major Menićanin explains the gunnery practice to the guests, while commander of the RV i PVO General Tus leans on the table. (M. Menićanin)

time, it was a privilege, since it was praised by the local politicians and party *nomenklatura*. However, in time of war it was to prove a dramatic challenge.

Training of the Air Base's Elements

200th Air Base operated and trained its units as any other air base in the RV i PVO. Generally, the training of combat units, such as 200th Infantry Company or 200th Light Air Defence Artillery Regiment were continuous and annual. The air base was actually engaged in many training activities outside the Bihać garrison.[12]

Conscript soldiers who served at the air base or any aviation units in Bihać received basic training for three months at 975th Air Training Centre at the air base at Sombor, near the Yugoslav-Hungarian border. The drivers were trained at 672nd (Air Force) Automobile Training Centre in Kovin – a former Luftwaffe air base. After initial training they were sent to Bihać and then distributed to the units, but underwent further training to accommodate duties in such a demanding environment. Generally, of 18 months – from mid-1980s 12 month – conscript period, the soldiers remained in Bihać for 12 – later nine months. Those who served in the aviation units or in the maintenance units of the Air Base actually carried out many of the important duties in the air base, from armourers, technicians, tractor and specialised vehicle drivers to updating information on the large perspex screens, alongside other typical duties such as guard and other general purpose work.[13] In general, conscripts were 'very well trained for carrying out their tasks, independent work on the technical devices, [and the] right handling and usage of the personal weaponry'.

In the event of war, 200th Air Base counted on the wider number of reservists that had served their conscript period in RV i PVO units, but in other air bases or aviation units. They would come from several municipalities of the Bihać region, mostly of Muslim or Serbian nationality. They were summoned to the units on an occasional basis during exercises, general inspections or at regular annual training. They had the chance to maintain their shooting proficiency but also to become accustomed to their war-time duties in the air base.

The aviation units did not count on reserve personnel, since their peace-time organisation structure almost the same as that in the event of war.

In 1983, 200th Air Base, including 236th Air Support Company at Prijedor air field, was fully mobilised in an exercise as the part of the checks carried out by the General Inspection of the People's Defence. It was marked with a "good" grade, which was the middle mark in the scale of the readiness markings.[14] In 1984, 200th Air Base took part in many activities including exercise "Tito's Drvar 84" supporting the light aviation at Medeno Polje and in the city of Drvar, and the joint tactical exercise "Plamen 84" at Udbina air base. The NBC Platoon passed 40 days of training at Manjača range south of Banja Luka.[15]

Most of the activities in 1985 took place prior to the visit of the federal Minister of Defence Admiral Branko Mamula to the air base. Exercise "Plamen" was repeated at the air base at Udbina along with activities at Manjača range.[16] 1986 saw live firing and training at the Slunj and Manjača ranges. In this year there were a lot of reserve personnel of the light air defence artillery regiment and the maintenance aviation units mobilised: around 82 percent of 67th Air Support Battalion and 262nd Air Support Company were reservists whilst up to 90 percent of other air base units were reserve soldiers, NCOs and officers. V Air Corps assessed 200th Air Base's training as achieving marks of 83-85 percent.[17]

Mobilisation checks in 1989 showed a slight decline in the response of the reserve cadres which ranged from 68 to 87 percent depending upon the time and duration of the exercise or check. The RV i PVO HQ marked 200th Air Base's combat readiness at 79.5 percent with a variety of markings ranging from 73 to 81 percent. In 1989, the Infantry Company deployed sections at Manjača and Slunj ranges.[18]

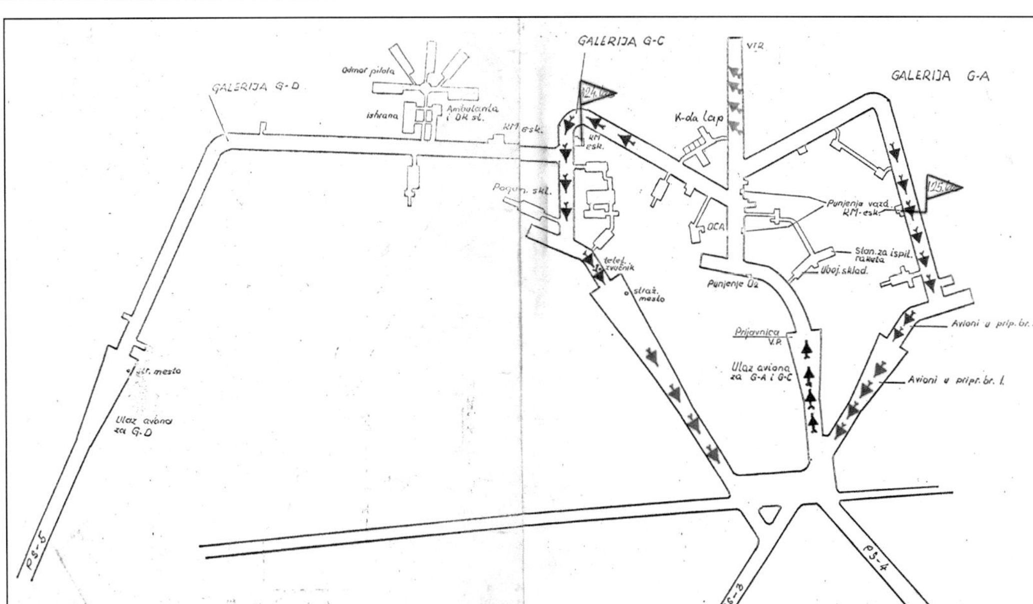

A plan of 117th Fighter Regiment's dispositions inside Objekt Klek. In the middle of the M-structured Objekt was the main entrance, Air Technical Workshop and the HQ of the regiment. On the left arm of the M was No. 124 Squadron, while on the right was No. 125 Squadron. Under this scheme dated in the mid-1980s, the aircraft in Combat Readiness No. 1 were located in front of the entrances of galleries A and C. Those which were in Combat Readiness No.2 were behind the protective doors, inside the Objekt. (D. Buban)

Objekt Klek

Objekt Klek was the core of Bihać Air Base. It had four entrances (marked as 1, 2, 3 and 4), nicknamed "holes", that connected the four underground galleries (A, B, C and D) which formed a structure looking somewhat like the letter "M". Inside, there were galleries for three MiG-21 squadrons and a technical workshop.

According to the initial manual for the usage of "Klek", from 1 May 1968, it was built to "secure the full autonomy of the units inside of the Objekt, [to enable] safe and continuous command of combat operations of the fighter regiment, continuous technical maintenance of the regiment even under ongoing attack by enemy aviation, [and maintain] normal conditions for the safety of the personnel. All of the performances of Objekt Klek [are to] maintain a high degree of intensity for preparation of the units for combat operations and maximal usage of the fighter aviation."[19]

Inside the Objekt there were premises of the HQ of 117th Fighter Regiment (117th Aviation Brigade in 1991/92) with offices for the commander, chief of staff and others of its assistants and sections (flying, personnel, technical, intelligence, etc).

Electric tug-tractors were used to take the MiGs out through the protected narrow exits ("usek") to the apron. Two APA-4 vehicles (APU) can be seen connected to this MiG-21F-13. The pilot is sitting in cockpit, as typical in the first days of Bihać Air Base in 1969. (HDA)

The Air Technical Workshop (known as "VTR" or *vazduhoplovna-tehnička radionica*) was an organisational part of 200th Air Base. It was tasked to carry out the so-called "third level of maintenance" for the MiG-21s of all of the squadrons at the base.

MiG-21PFM No. 22716, being towed out of the Objekt by an electric tug-tractor. (HDA)

Four Entrances

Each of the entrances (colloquially 'holes') had a massive, metal door that would be slid open during operations, and could be shut closed to protect the interior. Behind each door, at the beginning of each gallery, was another, even more massive armoured door. Those doors were closed on Fridays and re-opened on Monday morning at the start of the working week. Closing of the doors would follow the sounding of a siren. It was estimated that this part between the main entrance and the entrance of the gallery could absorb the effect of a nuclear explosion and enable regular operations to continue even after a nuclear detonation directly above the base and in front of an entry. The small corridors and galleries between the main entrances and the entrances to the galleries were built with the intention to receive and reduce a nuclear blast after a detonation in its vicinity or in front of the Objekt.

The doors were operated and moved by a combined electro/mechanical/hydraulic system. The protective doors at the entrances to galleries A, B and C were 20 metres wide, four metres high, 0.8 metres thick, weighed around 100 tonnes, and were powered by electrical motors. The doors for Gallery D were hydraulically-powered and measured 20 metres in width, nine metres in height, with a thickness of 0.6 metres, and covered the whole profile of the gallery.[20] Gallery D was not yet finished when the regiment moved in and thus a temporary – wooden – obstacle was in place at the entrance to the 'Roundabout' (see the reconstruction of Objekt Klek in the colour section for details).[21]

Early after the construction, the outside spaces between the entrances were empty and bare. Over the years the vegetation grew thus providing the best – natural – form of camouflage. In the beginning camouflage nets were used to hide the activities in front of the entrances, as obvious on enclosed photographs.

Underground Galleries

Each of the squadrons had its own – separate – gallery which could accommodate all of its aircraft. Gallery A was the home of No. 125 Squadron; Gallery C that of No. 124 Squadron, while Gallery D housed No. 352 Squadron. The maximum capacities of each of these galleries were as follows:

- A: 20 aircraft
- C: 22 aircraft
- D: 16 aircraft.

The main Maintenance Workshop was in Gallery B, in the centre of the Objekt, and could accommodate up to four to six MiGs, depending on the status of their disassembly, and whether their engines were removed or not.

Parking spots within the galleries were marked with red stripes. The length of the parking places in A and C galleries was 15 by 11 metres; in Gallery D it was 19 by 9 metres. In the galleries A and C the fighters were parked in staggered positions, while in Gallery D they were parked in column. The positions for the aircraft's nose-wheels and tug-tractors were marked in yellow and red on the floor. Additional – yellow – markings on the ground included walkways, and lockers for the most important tools and equipment for every aircraft. The work of the ground crews inside galleries was possible thanks to the installation of eight air conditioning chambers.

In the workshop, situated in Gallery B, the fighters were to be parked at a 21 degree angle off the main line and each position was marked in red.

Generally, the work in VTR was same as in any other regular Yugoslav air base, except for the higher security measures. At the beginning of the usage, it was planned that the door of the VTR should always be closed and it was also predicted that the engine checks would be carried out on the main apron in the times when no other aircraft were in the air or in the take-off phase. The maintenance of all vehicles – including electric tractors, was carried out outside of the Objekt.[22]

After a sortie and refuelling outside, three MiG-21s are towed back into the Objekt through main entrance B. (Author's collection)

Gallery A of No. 125 Squadron, as seen in 1969, with a line of MiG-21F-13s. (HDA)

Other Premises in the Objekt

There were numerous other premises in the Objekt to provide services. Those were:

- Control room with monitors used to control activities inside the Objekt and to give accurate information on air worthy and available MiGs at any given time.
- Operations Centre of 117th Fighter Regiment, and later jointly with 51st Air Surveillance Battalion, situated in the room marked G-K, with different perspex screens, showing the situation in the air, and flight calculations, reviews of air surveillance, air worthy aircraft, and the meteorological situation over the air base's area of responsibility and in the potential zones of operations, the NBC situation, tactical/technical details of enemy aircraft, and the markings of civil and airline aircraft. In the event of an emergency at the Operations Centre, a Combat Command Group was formed from the regimental CO, chief of staff, operations, intelligence officer and a number of other officers from Regimental HQ. The OC had all necessary documentation (orders of battle, operational diaries, communication schemes, charts, secret code names, ciphers, etc)
- The air traffic control and meteo-station. Initially they were situated in the Objekt at the G-K and G-T positions, but were later relocated to the new buildings outside the Objekt just near the apron.
- The technical centre located in room G-T was intended for monitoring and gathering facts and figures about the airworthy or combat ready aircraft, available parking space in the galleries and maintaining the indicators for information. It was tasked to maintain control and to provide correct information to

Armed with K-13 AAMs, a pair of MiG-21F-13s at the exit of Gallery A in 1969. (HDA)

Gallery C of No. 124 Squadron: a line of MiG-21Bis, seen in the mid-1980s. (N. Maravić family)

No. 352 Reconnaissance Squadron was located in Gallery D. Here, an electro tug-tractor tows a MiG-21F-13 in 1969. (HDA)

the personnel on displays and in the Operations Centre. The technical centre also ordered the opening or closure of the armoured doors at the entrances and controlled these activities through the television cameras at galleries and entrances/exits. They controlled the whole installation and warned the personnel of danger: fire was of great concern.

- The *Zvezda* ("Star") compartment, located aside from No. 352 Squadron's gallery. Known as the "star" due to its five rooms, it resembled the fingers of a five pointed half-star. This included the operations centre, a medical room where pre-flight checks were carried out, lockers for changing into flying suits, and classrooms for each of the three squadrons – separated only by wooden dividers – for the pilot pre-flight preparations and debriefs. A photo-laboratory and container room were also added where photo-camera films were developed, and aerial photo sections were made. There was also a kitchen and the mess: where officers (pilots) where served by the kitchen staff while NCOs took their meals separately. The Star's facilities were also used for rest, personal hygiene, and smoking – there were fixed lighters and ashtrays with water. In the event of war it was intended that the pilots remain in these rooms between their sorties.
- The armoury or armament storage – was tasked to receive the ordnance (missiles and gun ammunition) from the outside stores – where it was prepared, including assembly and testing, before turning over to the squadrons. The missiles were kept in this room and regularly checked on the test beds, usually after 25 hours spent on the pylons of the MiGs. The AAMs were kept on trailers for quick and easy access to the planes. They could also be ferried by the tractors, which originally followed a strictly defined route from the storage to each of the galleries. Some of the weapon preparation, such as for PLAB and napalm bombs, and missile engine checks were carried out outside the Objekt at marked locations. The main armament storage was outside the air base at Vedro Polje but a small section with sufficient missiles for regular needs was maintained within the Objekt.
- The other premises included: an aircraft battery power-station, fuel-storage with five large tanks/ reservoirs, and two generator compartments – diesel-electric power-stations I and II. There were nine air conditioning chambers (in nine rooms) each having a ventilation exit outside the Objekt. There were also exits for exhaust gases and "dirty air."

The ventilation exits above the Objekt were guarded with barbed wire, a permanent watch with dogs and were regularly patrolled. The watch posts had a telephone line to the watch barracks, and connected with the Technical Centre inside the Objekt. Electrical signal devices

A MiG-21F-13 (L-12) serial number 22512, as in service with 117th Fighter Regiment during the conversion of its elements to that type at Batajnica AB in the summer of 1968. The aircraft is shown armed with two R-3S missiles (colloquially known as 'K-13' in the RV i PVO, regardless their variant) on underwing pylons (one under each wing), a 490-litre drop-tank under the centreline, and equipped with SRO-2 IFF-antennae under the forward fuselage and atop the fin tip. (Artwork by Tom Cooper)

MiG-21U-400 (NL-12) serial number 22901 was the first example of this sub-variant acquired by the RV i PVO. It was re-assigned to 117th Fighter Regiment during its conversion to the type at Batajnica AB but was lost during transfer to Bihać AB on 9 August 1968. Its pilot, Captain 1st Class Jurinjak, was killed. The colour applied on these early two-seat MiG-21s was the same as applied to MiG-21F-13s and MiG-21PFMs. It consisted of two layers of clear lacquer mixed with 10% and 5% aluminium powder and was known colloquially as 'silver grey'. (Artwork by Tom Cooper)

During the 1970s 117th Fighter Regiment was re-equipped with MiG-21US. Amongst them was this example, serial number 22951, which was assigned to No. 352 Reconnaissance Squadron from 1981, and until scrapped under the Dayton Peace Accord at the Batajnica AB in 1997. As usual, the aircraft was painted in silver grey overall. Roundels were applied in four positions, with the full serial on the nose, the top right and bottom left of the wing. (Artwork by Tom Cooper)

MiG-21PFM (L-14) serial number 22704 of 117th Fighter Regiment, as seen during the Sloboda 71 exercise, run in October 1971, when it was one of several to wear the white 'lightning' insignia applied below the cockpit. The aircraft remained in service with No. 352 Reconnaissance Squadron at Bihać AB until May 1976. In 1993, it was returned to the unit when it was re-deployed to Batajnica AB but then scrapped three years later. It is shown with its standard armament of two R-3S air-to-air missiles only. (Artwork by Tom Cooper)

MiG-21PFM serial number 22719 of 117th Fighter Regiment was the only example of this variant to ever receive a camouflage pattern. This was applied during an overhaul at the Zmaj Works and consisted of the same BS381C/638 dark sea grey and BS381C/641 dark green on upper surfaces and sides, and PRU Blue on undersurfaces, as used on various locally manufactured aircraft types in Yugoslavia. While serving a tour with the HQ of 117th Regiment and then No. 125 Squadron for a while, this camouflage was never adopted for fleet-wide service, and even this aircraft as subsequently re-painted back to 'silver grey'. Shown under the centreline is the GP-9 pod for the 23mm twin-barrel GSh-23 gun. (Artwork by Tom Cooper)

Reaching Yugoslavia shortly after the MiG-21PFMs was the MiG-21R reconnaissance fighter variant, which received the local designation L-14i. This example was handed over to No. 352 Reconnaissance Squadron on 31 May 1971 and continued in service until its crash on 23 April 1986 when its pilot, Captain Šakota, was killed. Like the MiG-21F-13s and MiG-21PFMs before them, MiG-21Rs were originally painted in two layers of clear lacquer, but with a lower grade of aluminium powder, giving them a much lighter – though also 'patchier' – appearance: the latter factor was influenced by the milling methods and materials used to manufacture various sections of the skin. The aircraft is shown equipped with the N (night) photo-reconnaissance container, and a SAB bomblet for illumination of the target. (Artwork by Tom Cooper)

Initially acquired as interceptors, all the MiG-21bis (L-17s) of the JRV i PVO were painted in light grey overall, and received the usual set of national markings and serial numbers. This example, serial number 17110, was operated by No. 124 Squadron from 1978 until 1994, and is shown armed with an R-3R (ASCC/NATO-codename 'AA-2-2 Atoll') semi-active radar homing missile on the outboard pylon, and R-13M (ASCC/NATO-codename 'AA-2b Atoll') infra-red homing missile on the inboard pylon. The MiG-21bis 17110 was destroyed in an air strike on Nis AB during Operation Allied Force in 1999. (Artwork by Tom Cooper)

Compared with earlier variants, the MiG-21bis was a significantly improved 'multi-role' variant, which entered service with a wide range of air-to-air and air-to-ground weapons. This example, serial number 17111, was operated by No. 124 Squadron, from 1978 until a crash in 1987, after which it was scrapped. It is shown as armed with four Munja pods for 128mm unguided rockets. (Artwork by Tom Cooper)

The final MiG-21 variant to enter service with the JRV i PVO was the MiG-21bis-K (L-17K), most easily recognisable by the 'straight' edges of the sides of transparencies of its windshield. A further difference was that they had no antenna for the RSBN navigational system under the chin or the rear top of the fin. This example, serial number 17213, served with No. 125 Squadron at Bihać AB until withdrawn from there in late April 1992, and is shown armed with a pair of R-60MK (ASCC/NATO-codename 'AA-8 Aphid') infra-red homing missiles on the outboard underwing pylons, and one R-13M on the inboard underwing pylon. 17213 was destroyed during an air strike on Nis AB in the course of Operation Allied Force in May 1999. (Artwork by Tom Cooper)

MiG-21bis (L-17) serial number 17126 served with No. 125 Squadron of 117th Fighter Regiment from 1988 until 1992. It is shown as it appeared early during the war in the former Yugoslavia, still wearing its full insignia, and armed with the British-made Hunting BL.755 CBU (usually installed on the inboard underwing pylon). The aircraft survived not only the wars of 1991-1995, but also some combat damage it suffered from an air strike during Operation Allied Force in 1999, and remained in service until at least 2006. Inset is shown the insignia of the Zmaj Works, applied on all aircraft overhauled there. (Artwork by Tom Cooper)

Early during the War in Yugoslavia, in the summer of 1991, the High Command JRV i PVO ordered the removal of 'squadron numbers' (the large black serials applied on the forward fuselage, top of the right and bottom of the left wing) from all of its aircraft. This, and intensive flying resulted in the worn-out appearance of this MiG-21bis, serial number 17109, which had served with No. 124 Squadron of 117th Fighter Regiment from Bihać AB since June 1978. On 18 September 1991, this jet was claimed as shot down by Croatian forces while being flown by Captain Mandić, who ejected safely but was captured. It is shown armed with a pair of R-3Rs and four R-60MKs. (Artwork by Tom Cooper)

MiG-21R (L-14i) serial number 26111 was operated by No. 352 Reconnaissance Squadron of 117th Fighter Regiment from late May 1971 until 11 April 1992, when it was claimed as shot down by Croatian forces in the Kupres area: its last pilot, Captian Grandić, was captured. It is shown in its final appearance, painted in a highly polished overall finish very similar to the silver dope of British origin; with 490-litre underwing drop-tanks in light grey, and carrying the D (day) photo-reconnaissance pod under the centreline. (Artwork by Tom Cooper)

The Yugoslav Minister of Defence, Admiral Branko Mamula, as seen during an inspection of Bihac AB in 1985. This photograph was taken inside the Operations Centre, and shows Mamula accompanied by Lieutenant-Colonel Vladeta Kostić, contemporary commander of 117th Fighter Regiment. (B. Pejić)

Two young pilots of No. 352 Squadron – Šušić and Rajlić – as seen after donning their VKK-4 high altitude g-suits, and while the technicians help them fix their GSh-4 helmets, in 1969 or 1970. (Author's collection)

A view down Gallery A, with MiG-21PFMs of No. 125 Fighter Squadron, in the mid-1970s. (MC Odbrana)

Ground crew working on a MiG-21F-13 inside Objekt Klek, in 1969 or 1970. (Author's collection)

Winter flying day at Bihać AB, sometime in the mid-1980s: visible are a MiG-21R and ground crew of No. 352 Reconnaissance Squadron. (Miloš Vukojević)

Summer flying day, 19 June 1985: two MiG-21R (26109 and 26103) equipped with D reconnaissance containers, are visible in the foreground, while the MiG-21UM (22953) is prepared for take-off in the rear. (M. Vukojević, S Janjanin)

Refuelling MiG-21Bis 17213 at the 'Usek' in front of Entrance B. Notably, the jet is hooked up to an electric tug-tractor. (117 LAP via P. Grandić)

Armourers fixing a GSh-23 underbelly gun prior to loading 23mm ammunition. Clearly visible in the upper left foreground is an UB-16-57 pod for 57mm S-5K unguided rockets. (Author's collection)

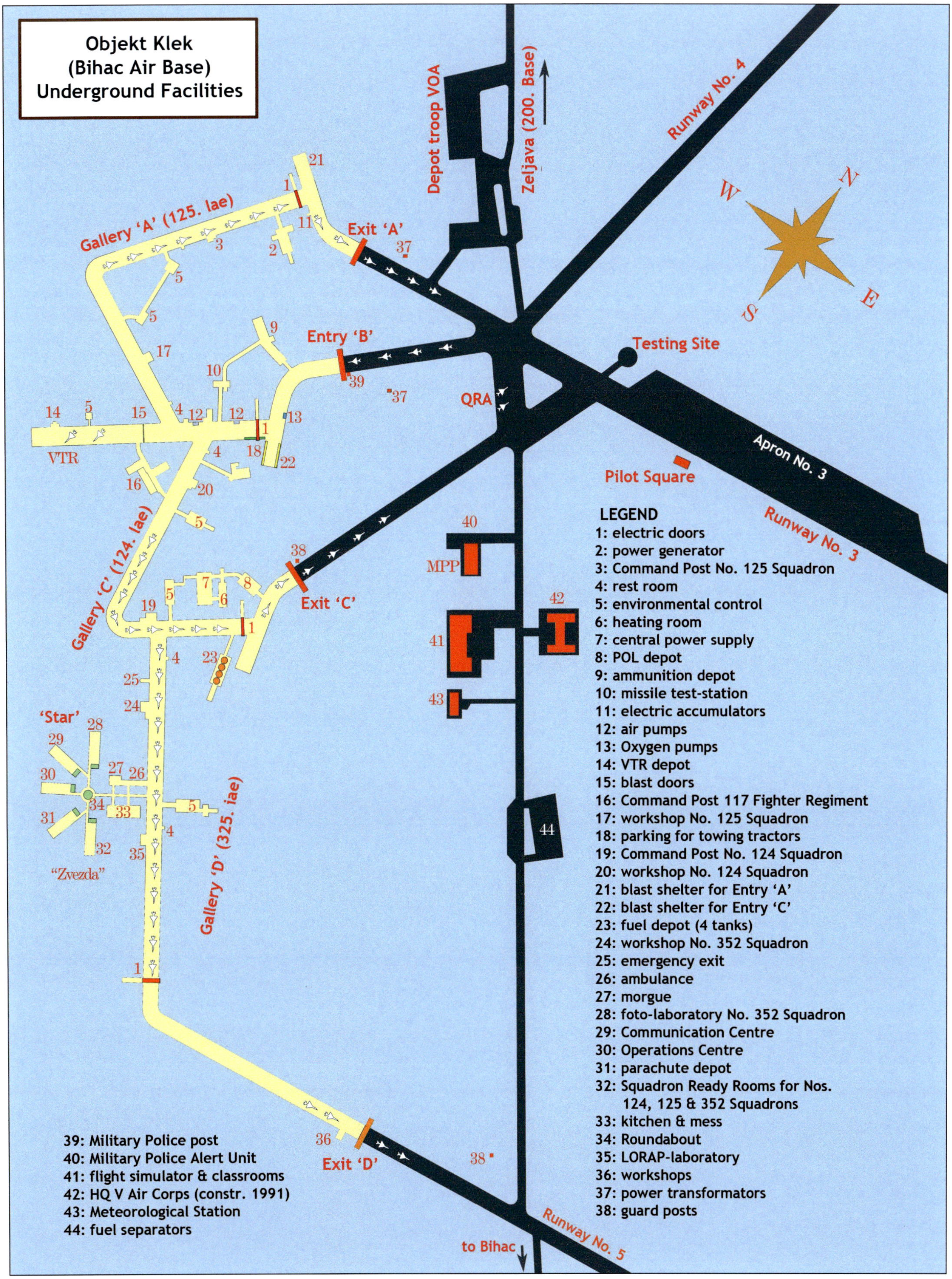

A reconstruction of Objekt Klek, with all underground facilities marked in yellow. (Courtesy Predrag Grandić)

A map of the complete 200th Air Base, including all five of its runways, the underground Objekt Klek (marked in violet); and the view of one of its main entries. (Author's collection)

Maintenance and after-flight checks were carried out in the galleries, as it was the case with this MiG-21PFM. (Author's collection)

The inscription on the wall of Gallery B orders "Greasy cloths, waste fuel and oil [should be] immediately take[n] out from the gallery." (HDA)

Gallery B accommodated the Air Technical Workshop of 200th Air Base. Tito's quotes adorned the entrance. (HDA)

Gallery B was projected to accommodate up to four MiG-21s. (Author's collection)

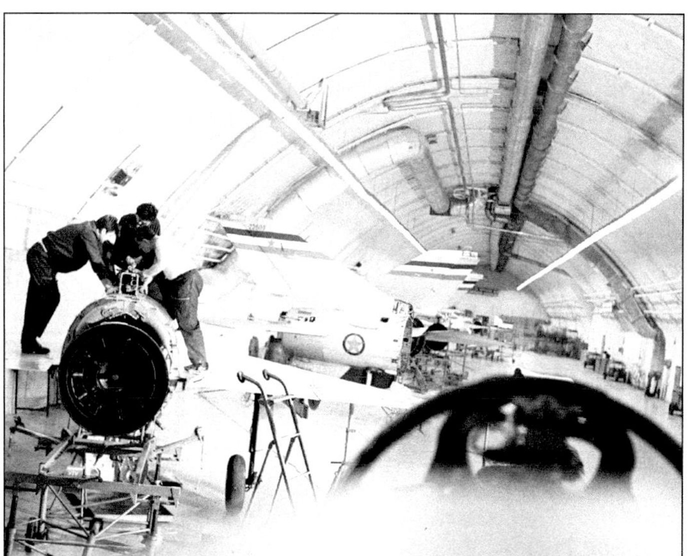

The Air Technical Workshop inside Objekt Klek carried out "third level" maintenance. It included the larger repairs, exchange of engine and other works. (HDA)

Technicians seen while working on MiG-21U No. 22908. This airframe was nicknamed "Skylab" by pilots and it served 117th Regiment for over twenty years. (via Ranko Kovačević)

on fences were later introduced in addition to the military police observation posts.

The Objekt was equipped with loudspeakers connected in "10 sound circles" and the system was used to announce orders or commands, to alert, inform or call personnel, and to order take off. There was also system of radio communications inside of the Objekt.[23]

From the middle of the Objekt/Gallery C there was the elevator which accessed to a control tower 60 metres higher than the ground level of the Objekt. The Air Traffic Control premises were built into the

Scenes from the Operations Room, located some 50-60 metres above the galleries, from where flying was controlled: colonels Tus and Bračun of 15th Air Defence Division monitor the flying. (Branislav Bajić)

Lt Col Janjanin controls the flying day of No. 352 Squadron. (S. Janjanin)

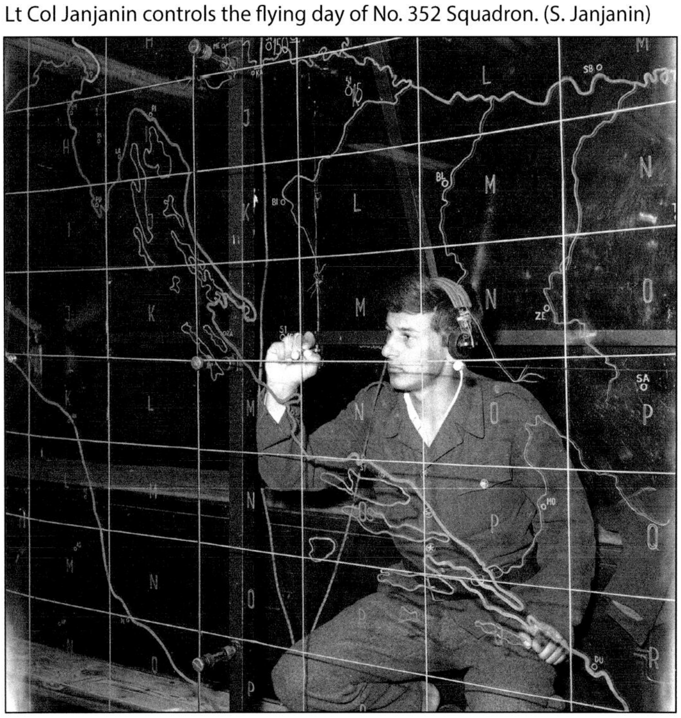

A soldier marking one of the large perspex screens, referred to as "planchettes," in the Operations Centre. (HDA)

Inside the Technical Centre which monitored all of the activities inside the Objekt via TV cameras. (HDA)

rock above the Objekt and from that position it was possible to observe the main part of the runways and taxiways and the view stretched almost all the way to the city of Bihać on the eastern side. Air Traffic Controllers worked during the day and during flying. Later, between entrances 3 and 4 a new building was constructed to accommodate the Federal Department for Air Traffic Control servicemen and another was built for the meteorological section. Civilians were employed and tasked to provide support for flying and in pre-flight preparations one from each of those services would be engaged to brief the pilots on the situation.

In the autumn of 1991, a separate building outside the Objekt was built to accommodate V Air Corps that had evacuated from Zagreb.

Security measures inside the Objekt

From the beginning of its existence personnel were warned that "all facts concerning the Objekt Klek and its usage are of STRICTLY CONFIDENTIAL NATURE". It was explained that: "Because of its utmost importance for the defence of the State, this Objekt represents

Pilot classroom, 1969. (HDA)

A relaxed flight preparation in the classroom of No. 352 Squadron in 1970. Note the poster showing the roundels of foreign air forces. (HDA)

Flight preparation led by Major Krivokapić, CO of No. 125 Squadron, in 1975. The pilots are dressed in VKK-6 high altitude equipment. (MC Odbrana)

special interest and [is] the aim of foreign intelligence attacks, which should always remain in sight." Security of the Objekt would be strictly maintained through the application of measures, procedures

Flight preparation in No. 352 Reconnaissance Squadron during the mid-1980s. The pilots wear Yugoslav flight gear. Note the walls painted in the light blue to prevent clouds of dust. (M. Popovic)

"Political education", according to the poster on the wall, in the one of the classrooms in the Objekt. The walls were still unpainted when this photograph was taken. (M. Popovic)

Fo13209 Ca-41
ser. i br. leg. ser. i br. prop.
kap. I klase
(čin)
BUBAN
(prezime)
Petar
(očevo ime)
DUŠAN
(ime)
15.01.1990.g.
(datum izdavanja)
Overava

A typical ID for entrance into the Objekt as issued in 1990. (D. Buban)

and limitations issued in the instructions of May 1968 for each of the facilities and working places.

The secrecy of the Objekt was maintained through the detailed analyses of the biographies and later behaviour of the personnel that would serve there. A written obligation to preserve the secrecy of all facts and figures related to the Objekt was mandatory and remained even after a transfer to another air base, unit or leaving the service, whether active or conscript. It was immediately perceived that Objekt Klek was sensitive to demolition or sabotage attacks from an enemy. "It was of extreme need to preserve in secrecy tactical/technical facts

A soldier wearing an arm-band with the letters DP, indicating that he is on day duty. (HDA)

on [the] Objekt, specific technical solutions, working possibilities, command capacities and life of the units in the Objekt."

When the Objekt was first in use, the movement of personnel and time spent in certain parts of the Objekt were to be strictly controlled and monitored by unit commanders or the officers on duty. It was also ordered that all doors should be kept closed, and only opened to allow aircraft to move to the aprons. Passes were issued for different part of the Objekt, which limited personnel access to areas or rooms only linked to their duties. Security officers would inform personnel not to talk about the underground Objekt to non-authorised persons outside the air base.

Generally, most of the personnel were not interested the business of others or in areas outside their responsibilities and this attitude was taken as standard behaviour. The pilots were not interested in ground crew business. The technicians were not interested in the pilots' jobs and missions. The conscript soldiers were tasked with their own duties and were usually not allowed to "cruise" in the Objekt if they were not ordered to do so. Those who served in the Engineer or Air Surveillance Battalion were not allowed to enter the Objekt or nearby aprons. Those who were in the structure of the air base limited their movements only to duties that they were tasked to do. The regime of movement was strict in the early days of the Objekt and air base's usage. However, it seems that over the years the movements in the base and behaviour at the aprons started to be more relaxed even though the rules remained strict.

Fire prevention was one of the most serious tasks concerning the security of the Objekt. Utmost importance was given to prevent any possibility of fire inside the Objekt and "matches, lighters, firearms, photo cameras and alcohol" were banned. All personnel were subjected to search and confiscation of the prohibited items and were strictly warned on procedures to avoid any flame or fire. The taking of any flammable or forbidden devices was punishable.[24] Lieutenant Colonel Tepšić recalled that the military police at the entrance were tasked to check that personnel should not take any flammable device into the Objekt. Fire-fighters were ordered to react immediately and at any price to stop any spread of fire inside the Objekt.[25] The workshop was strictly limited in what activities it could undertake in order to prevent accidents or possible fire.

In the galleries it was forbidden to tow aircraft in the opposite direction to that prescribed, to turn them around inside the Objekt, to load or clean guns, unload the remaining fuel from reservoirs, to fill the aircraft with oxygen, to use any flammable devices, to smoke or to dine in the galleries.

In addition to the Operations Centre, which was permanently working, there was an "on duty" system inside the Objekt which included permanent "on-duty" servicemen at the Technical Centre, a technical officer of the Objekt, a section for technical maintenance of the Objekt, teams at the apron and entrance, fire-fighters, shifts of military police, tug-tractor drivers, and the "deponage team" (crash-landing team). It was planned that all personnel "on duty" would carry a standard red band on the right arm, but with the different letters ("DO", "DTC" or at galleries: "DS-A", C, D or for the drivers "V") indicating the location of their duty, and the importance of their position.

At any given time, there was a military fire-fighting team, and a civilian team consisting of technicians tasked with monitoring and maintaining various installations inside the Objekt: the latter was responsible for maintaining the air conditioning, power supply, thermostats and hydrostats, ventilators, heating room, pumps, valves and diverse other instruments, and worked in shifts lasting eight hours. The same maintenance team was tasked with organising and controlling the transfer of fuel into the tanks inside the underground facility, as well as to the depot outside the Objekt.

A special plan was developed in the event that the main doors had to be closed in emergency: the corresponding order had to be issued by the CO of 117th Regiment, and resulted in measures being taken to protect air conditioning and ventilation, activate generators, and ensure an autonomous water supply.

Another plan envisaged the masking of the Objekt with camouflage elements and nets, and with vegetation planted around the nearby taxiways and down the mountain atop of the underground facility. It was also planned to paint the taxiways, construct dummy entrances and deploy decoy aircraft in the event of a war – even though there is no evidence that this was ever actually done.

No sidearms were allowed inside the Objekt – regardless of rank or function – with only one exception: pilots heading to or returning from combat sorties. In between the sorties they were obliged to keep their sidearms in lockers.

How the Objekt operated

Each morning a column of 18 to 24 military coaches was parked in the centre of Bihać, where they would be boarded by the personnel of the units of the air base en route to start their daily shift.[26] Each bus was to carry personnel from a specific unit, although most of the men used to live in the flyer's housing within the Harmani estate. Nicknamed simply 'the column', this was organised along a very strict hierarchy: the CO of 200th Air Base was in the first coach, and the commanding officer of every other unit had to take a seat next to the driver of his bus – followed by his deputy, assistants, subordinated officers, pilots and technicians depending on their ranks. Tepšić recalled that the pilots were privileged to sit in front of ground crews in the respective squadron coaches.

After passing several checkpoints on its way, the column would reach the base, distributing personnel to their squadron-entrances into the Objekt: the personnel of the air base and other ground units continued to their barracks in Željava.[27]

Arming the MiGs with K-13 AAMs was common practice in early stages of Objekt Klek's usage. (HDA)

Entrance into the Objekt was allowed only through entrance B (2), while A (1), C (3) and D (4) were exclusively exits for aircraft. The MiGs from No. 125 Squadron were taken out of the Objekt through entrance 1, while those from No. 124 Squadron used entrance 3. No. 352 Squadron used entrance 4. Exit at the end of working hours was strictly through B (2).

At the main entrance, or "hole", there was a small kiosk which housed military police. They were tasked to monitor the entrance and to allow entrance only to approved personnel. Entrance and exit was allowed only with issued passes. In the early days of usage personnel were distinguished by the colour of the identification cards worn on the chest of the uniform above their rank markings. After the first half of the 1970s this practice was abandoned and personnel would leave their identification card with the guards at the kiosk when they entered the Objekt for the first time in the morning and these were returned back at the end of the working hours.

Inside each gallery were positions for aircraft and installations for refuelling. At the sides of the galleries there were additional fuel tanks, MiG radome covers and drawbars. The lights were dimmed, except when works or checks were being carried out on aircraft on "technical days". Generally, for most of the period galleries were in the dark, with lights only at the entrances and crossroads between the galleries. The Workshop was excused, since there were works on the aircraft.

The MiGs were prepared inside the Objekt and all of the pre-flight and post-flight checks were carried out inside the galleries. The aircraft were to be armed in the area between entrance and taxiway, literally known as the *usek* ("cut"). The APU or fuel tanks were also there to provide for the launch of certain aircraft. Each of the MiGs was in the charge of a technical NCO who had the main responsibility over the plane. The other technicians included those who took care of the radar, radio, and electronics of each aircraft.

In the gallery there was a refuelling system with a station for each aircraft. The system had a light which marked if the aircraft was refuelled or not and showing that aircraft was prepared. This information was visible at the operations centre, though this system was abandoned later and was no longer used. Nobody thought of the effects that fuel exhaust or vapor may have upon the health of the personnel or possibility of fire. Up to the war of 1991, only QRA aircraft were armed inside the Objekt: between 1987 and 1992 no arming of the MiGs was allowed inside the Objekt.

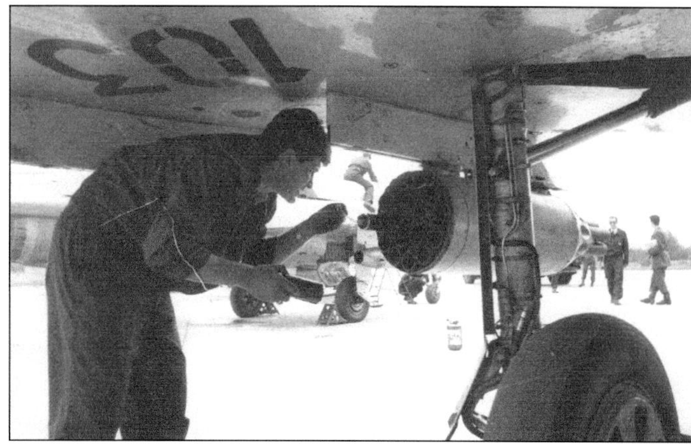

For most of the life-span of Bihać air base, the arming of the MiGs was carried outside of the Objekt. Here, a UB-16-57 unguided rocket pod is armed on MiG-21R No. 26103. (Nebojša Novaković)

All of the arming of aircraft was done on the apron. Over the years, there were few incidents with the loading of armament, guided or unguided rockets on the apron. In the summer of 1990, an incident occurred in No. 125 Squadron, one underbelly GSh-23 gun round ricocheted and killed young Sergeant Marjan Veličkovski. This was the only fatality under such circumstances during the operation of the air base.

After the first testing, it was decided that the MiGs should not be fuelled and prepared inside the Objekt. There were trials with direct roll-outs from the gallery, via the entrance, to the runway. The smoke from the jet engine exhaust remained in the gallery for days, meaning that the ground crews breathed in the exhaust. This also meant that the wingman's aircraft could not be started due to the lack of oxygen and massive exhaust cloud.

There was an intensive conversion course for all newcomer technicians, officers or NCOs. At the end of the course, each of them would be examined by a demanding three member commission, gathered from senior technicians in the base. Those who were sent to the 117th Regiment would then join the "I level" of maintenance within the squadrons; meaning work on the apron. The MiGs were in

The "first degree" of maintenance, was carried out on the apron in front of the Objekt, as was the case with this MiG-21PFM. (via B. Pejic)

Yugoslav-made electric EKV-250S tug-tractors were used between 1979 and 1992 for towing aircrafts inside and outside of the Objekt. (R. Djurić)

A technician from No. 352 Squadron takes the AFA-39 camera out from the container on a MiG-21R. (Krila armije)

The corridors between preparation classrooms and the galleries where the MiGs were kept were extremely narrow. (HDA)

the charge of the Air Technical Company of each squadron, under its first platoon nicknamed as the "mechanics", with each aircraft having its own NCO mechanic who was responsible for it. The 2nd platoon of the technical company were the "armourers" (2nd) and – loosely translated – the 3rd were the "equipmenters". Since the armourers had fewer daily duties than the standard mechanics they were mostly used as the drivers for the tractor tugs inside the Objekt. As Tepšić recalls, most of the mechanics who were responsible for an aircraft preferred not to allow to somebody else to tow "their" MiG outside the Objekt where the daily routine continued.[28]

The MiGs tasked to fly on a particular day were taken out in the order that they were parked inside the gallery. The towing was carried out by the NCOs of all specialties except for the mechanics from the regiment or Reconnaissance Squadron who specialised in engines and fuselages. The aircraft would be towed by tug-tractors up to their position outside the Objekt.

An aircraft which was not tasked to fly, or had different, mostly smaller, malfunctions would also be taken outside, driven in a semi-circle and returned back in the gallery for further preparations or work. If the malfunction was larger it was driven to the gallery where the workshop was situated. Those with larger malfunctions or with a need for regular overhauls were ferried to Air Depot "Zmaj" in Velika Gorica, Zagreb. In such cases, a technician who had his MiG in the workshop or at the Air Depot, had a period of less intensive work and would be ordered to other duties or the reserve of the squadron.

Up until 1979 the "yellow" electric tractors were built in Bulgaria. New tug-tractors arrived in 1979 and the old Bulgarian ones were passed on to Priština air base.[29] The "grey" EKV-250S tractors were built by the Rade Končar enterprise in Zagreb and the gearbox was built by TAM in Maribor. Most were painted in standard Yugoslav olive drab colour but two of them painted in blue were assigned to Objekt Klek's HQ and one painted in red was used by the fire-fighting unit. Inside the Objekt there were stations where four tractor batteries could be powered. The other type of tractor, the EKS-1001, was not so common in usage at Bihać Air Base – according to some sources there were two of these with 200th Air Base. Electric tractors were used to tow the MiGs up to a line painted on the ground just outside the entrances. Then, standard tractors built by IMT (Massey Fergusson) and driven by conscript soldiers would take over and tow the aircraft to the apron.

A similar pattern was used to return the MiGs to the Objekt with the main difference being that the air mechanic who was in charge of a particular aircraft would sit in the cockpit and could react or press the breaks in case of any problems. The NCOs would take-over at the line

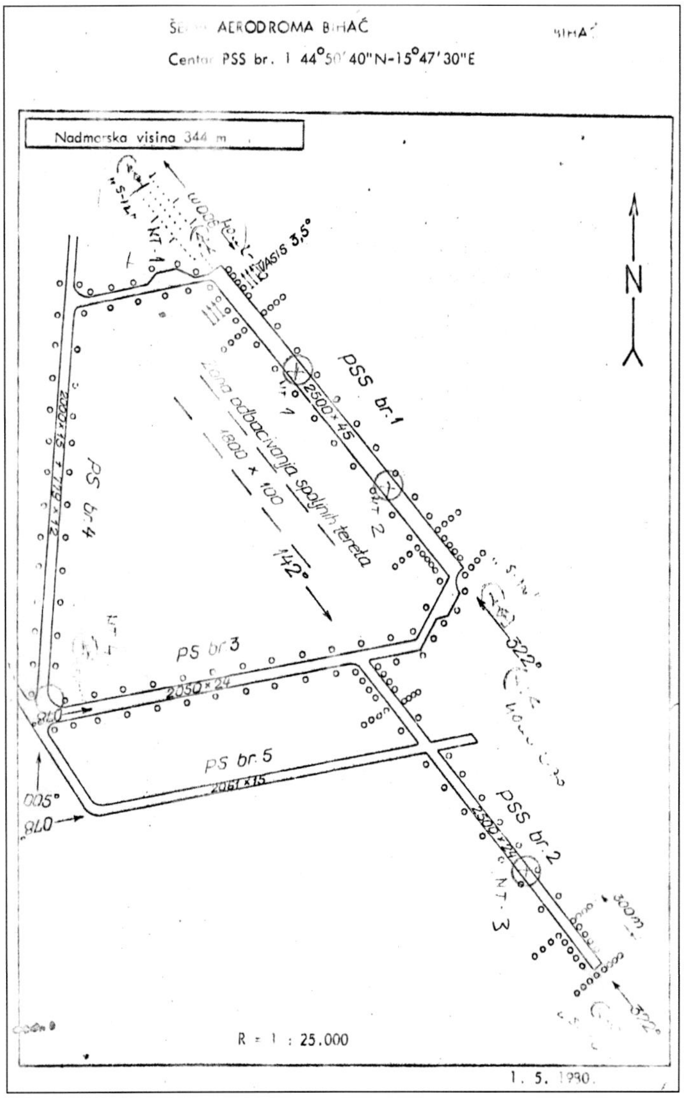

Scheme of the taxiways and main runways. (D. Buban)

and return the aircraft to the Objekt. It was a unique practice that the NCOs and technical officers would drive tractors and was necessary since precision in towing the MiGs inside the Objekt was demanding. The return of MiGs from the QRA position was carried out directly with electric tractors.

While inside the Objekt pilots remained in the "Star" most of the time. There were lockers for flying suits, dining facilities, and each of the squadrons had a classroom where flight preparations and other official gatherings were held. Pilots generally remained away from the apron until their aircraft were prepared and would then arrive at the aircraft designated for that day. It was similar after a flight, the pilot would simply leave the cockpit and continue to the squadron offices for debrief.

Flying from Bihać Air Base

Monday was a "technical day", while the "flying days" were Tuesday, Wednesday and Thursday, and Friday was a "reserve flying day" if the meteo-conditions meant that one of the regular flying days had been skipped. At Bihać Air Base this was a frequent case, since the meteo-situation was subject to sudden changes of the weather, though flying on Fridays was generally avoided, since a decline was noted in the attention of pilots prior to the weekend. The biorhythms of each pilot were carefully monitored and this also influenced the daily flying schedule.

As Tepšić recalls, in this period flying was organised into four daily sorties (literally – "the exits") or two day plus two night sorties. When night flying was organised, the working hours were moved to late afternoon and night and the coach from the city started at 17:00 hours. Flying started at dusk, continuing into the night, usually finishing between 23:00 and 00:00 hours. Work on the aprons was carried out under the reflectors, and with usage of the flashlights carried by the technicians. Night flying would continue on the following night, or there would be 2+2 day/night sorties, or if it was Friday when no further flying was scheduled.

During the "flying day" technicians would carry out three types of checks: before, in-between and after the flight. Pilots usually prepared for the sortie away from the apron and arrived at the assigned aircraft, received a report from the technicians, made their checks, entered the cockpit and took off. A usual sortie would last 25-30 minutes, or rarely, 40 minutes.[30]

One of No. 352 Squadron's pilots, Suad Hamzić explained that pilots used runways Nos. 4, 3 and 5, from west to east, only for taking off. Runway No. 3 connected the Objekt with both main runways PSS-1 and PSS-2 and it was wider than runways No. 4 and No. 5. Runway No. 4 was the longest and it turned into a road which connected the air base and the local road between Bihać (east) and village of Rakovica (west).

PSS No. 5 was parallel with PSS No. 3, but it was narrow, with even more narrow safety areas. Taking off from it was like taking off from an aircraft carrier, since just after 100 meters from its end was the start of the ridge of the plateau where the air base was located. The very unpopular PSS No. 5 was an extension of underground Gallery C.[31] The popular "Rolba" snow-clearer, mounted on a Mercedes Benz Unimog and later to some other types, were used for clearing the snow from runways. For drying the wet runway, an improvised heater made from a Tumansky R-11F-300 engine and fitted to a trailer would be used. The three-wheel trailer was then towed all over the runway until it was dry to enable safe flying.[32]

The aircraft would start its engine and taxi using runway No. 3, up to main runway No. 2 and then took off. Sometimes runway No. 4 would be used, but it was mostly used by the QRA pair for quick take offs. Runway No. 5 was very rarely used for taking off. On each side of the runway were natural holes and gusts or sudden changes of wind direction could be a real challenge for taxing and landing and there was a danger that a MiG would slide into one of these holes.

Wild animals were occasional and unusual guests and would trespass onto the runways and taxiways, especially in the early years and into the 1970s. A later commanding officer of 117th Regiment remembers that during the preparation for flying in the mid-1970s his group of pilots saw a bear crossing PSS-2. In another case a two-seater MiG struck a roe deer during take-off.[33]

Most of the "flying" activities took place outside the Objekt on the so-called "Triangle". At the beginning of the usage of the Objekt, it was planned that each squadron would maintain QRA pairs at their respective exits (A, C and D). Their back-up MiGs were to be located inside the Objekt at the end of the galleries, in front of the armoured doors parked in column one by one, with their pilots in the squadron rooms. Throughout the day the MiGs were ready at the apron. In case of alert, the pilots who were on QRA duty, rushed from the nearby premises to the cockpit and immediately took off using runway No. 4 (0-5). MiGs on QRA were taken into the Objekt at night, but remained on the inner side of the entrances with their radomes almost touching the doors.

The QRA take-off signal was usually given by the Operations Centre of the 15th Division PVO. After February 1986 this was replaced by

As it should be: QRA team awaits the alert call. (Author's collection)

As it really was: QRA pilots "killing time" playing cards and chess (N. Šušić)

the Operations Centre of 51st Air Surveillance Battalion/5th Air Surveillance Regiment. The take-off order was given by telephone and was also supposed to use the loudspeakers or light signal to scramble the pilots. The operations officer on duty would inform the Air Surveillance/divisional OC of the pilot's call sign, the position where the fighter was heading to intercept the enemy formation or aircraft and the channel for communications with the fighter during the sortie.

The flying was controlled by the regimental Operations Centre. It operated at the permanent base around the clock and consisted of the operations officer of the day, the chief of the shift and a group tasked with reviewing the situation in the air space and guidance.[34]

The MiGs were taken out from exits A, C and D to the QRA position or to the apron, where they were then organised. The take-off party consisted of a commander, the mechanic of the particular aircraft

Pre-flight meteorological preparation was carried out by the civil meteorologist that worked alongside the traffic control. (M. Matančić)

Pilots usually waited for their turn/sortie outside the Objekt under the watchful eye of the squadron CO. (S. Janjanin)

Early days: ground crew in proper order, full gear and coloured ID passes above their rank insignia, waiting for the return of their MiGs. (M. Popović)

Mid-1980s: much relaxed ground crew, even with the photographer present, wait for their aircraft. (M. Popović)

Two K-13 armed MiG-21PFMs along with APAs at the "Usek", covered with camouflage nets, prior to take off. (HDA)

and inform the operations centre that aircraft were ready (or not) for sortie. Each of the flying days had a main and a reserve flying plan. The pilots would be informed on the weather situation by the meteorologist – who was usually civilian, and often a woman (which proved popular with the pilots).

At the beginning of the flying day a weather reconnaissance flight was carried out by a single pilot. After his return, flying would start and depending upon the mission or weather, continued during the day or night. After pre-flight preparations, the pilots would be outside the Objekt and mostly gathered near the apron. In the early days they were simply left sitting on the grass or improvised seats. Later on, small huts were built near the taxiways where pilots of each squadron gathered. These huts were not allowed originally since the surrounding was bare and without any vegetation and it was concluded that such pilot huts would give away the position of the base. As the trees and bushes grew, and the air base became widely known, it was decided that pilots' huts near the taxiways should be built to improve the conditions and enable pilots to relax while waiting for their sortie. Eventually, even pre-flight briefings were run in these huts, usually by the squadron CO.

which was ordered to serve in QRA or to fly that day, the armourer, and ground crew who drove the tractors, and an auxiliary power unit (known as 'APA', usually mounted on ZIL-131 or Ural-375 lorries). There would be additional equipment, such as cockpit stairways, vehicle chocks, and fire-extinguishers in this area. The team was tasked to wait for the pilot, start up the engine, prepare the ordnance

Refuelling after a flight at the "Usek" in front of Entrance B in 1986. (117.lap via P. Grandic)

Flying from Bihać Air Base was very difficult as most of the contemporaries judged. Sometimes, it resembled operating from an aircraft carrier on the sea. One veteran pilot recalled:

Flying day is over: returning to the galleries. (HDA)

> The meteorological conditions in the vicinity of the air base, added to the modest ground and navigation equipment of the base and aircraft themselves, represented a serious problem, sometimes directly leading to the insecurity to the safety of the pilots. The slopes of Plješevica, other mountains and Čelopek hill just a few kilometres prior to the edge of the landing runway frequently resulted in limited visibility and low base of clouds. It was not a problem in excellent visibility, except when the wind blew which caused strong "pitching" in the approaching phase... We had the opportunities to see that between the beginning and the end of the runway winds blew from three different sides. I saw a MiG-21 after take-off when wind, actually the local turbulence over Klokot creek in the area of runway No. 1, turned it as if it was made of paper. I have seen a storm which closed the air base in a matter of a few minutes, with heavy showers, storm and hurricane-like winds. The narrow safe strips were not forgiving of the mistakes of the pilots. Any turn from the main direction during take-off or landing on some of the runways had been paid for dearly.[35]

Night flying was a frequent and very demanding activity. Usually, during night flying, the Objekt and air base signalling system would switch to generators ("DIT") which were situated at near the entrances 1 and 3. This was mandatory practice since it was not acceptable that some malfunction in the civil electric network could jeopardise the flying.

The return of the aircraft required a very strict procedure. Runway No.1 was used for landing, and a landing party would wait for the MiGs on the apron, in front of entrance B. The most serious issue was always the deactivation of the armament, such as missiles, unguided rockets, gun ammunition, that was brought back, and the regulation of oxygen. The responsible technicians were ordered to check the systems of their aircraft, and if any problem arose to send it to the workshop. The loading of oxygen and fuel was carried out at the entrance of gallery B, prior to taking the fighters into their galleries.

If there were any problems the aircraft was ordered to stop at the junction between runways No. 3 and No. 1, where this would usually be solved. Then the aircraft would taxi up to entrance No. 2, where it was refuelled, empty oxygen bottles replaced, and then the aircraft was towed away into the gallery for further checks and preparation for a new sortie. Each of the squadrons had a few experienced pilots who conducted test flights of the MiGs that had undergone repairs at the VTR workshop. After such test flights the MiG would be approved (or not) for further flying within the squadrons.

Any aircraft brought into the Objekt first had to stop its engine and shut down all of its electric systems before being towed inside by an electric tractor. The latter would first bring the aircraft to the red-marked 'line of shutting down the engine', in front of entrance B. Inside the galleries, the aircraft were parked in a zig-zag pattern, to leave as much free space as possible to their side. A typical flying day would be closed with a flight debrief in the squadron ready room, preparation for the next flying day (if any), changing from flying suits to standard uniforms, and – after the working hours – boarding the coaches that would bring the personnel back to their homes in Bihać.

Theory days did not involve flying and were usually run when the weather was unsuitable for flying. There were also routine written exams on proceedures, then working with the younger pilots, information gathering, meetings of the KPJ, and classes in political sciences – the latter being rather boring and unpleasant experiences, often lasting for hours. One of the veterans of Bihać Air Base, Danijel Borović recalled that after leaving the base for annual holidays, different courses, or temporary duty elsewhere, and then returning to the 'Hole', it took time to acclimatise to the underground Objekt again, its light blue walls, and artificial light. Rather unsurprisingly, pilots generally tried to spend most of their time outside, and sport activities – like playing football or volleyball – were enthusiastically pursued by many. On the other hand, technicians – especially those from the workshop, photo-laboratories, containers, armament sections, and all of those who were on other duties – were accustomed to pulling their shifts in the Objekt.

4

Bihać Air Base at War: 1991–1992

The announcement of the forthcoming war in the vicinity of the air base happened in spring of 1991. The position of Bihać Air Base between two republics and in an area populated by Serbs, Croats and Muslims was in Tito's era a sign of the proclaimed policy of the 'Brotherhood and Unity' of all the Yugoslav ethnic groups. However, after the democratic elections in Croatia there came a shift of political power from Communists to the Croatian Democratic Union, which pursued a nationalist ideology. This political change caused political, and later armed, resistance in the Serb populated areas of Croatia. The new authorities eagerly took measures to deploy their police forces and later also the Croat National Guard (Zbor Narodne Garde, ZNG), in those areas.

Spring 1991: On the Frontline

Most of the villages on the Croatian side of the air base, including Željava, Ličko Petrovo Selo and others were populated by Serbs. Their militias constructed numerous checkpoints and outposts along the local roads. The first clashes took place when the Croats attempted to move in their ZNG troops in April 1991. The establishment of a Croat police station in the village of Željava was prevented by the military police from the air base: this would have been positioned literally inside the perimeter. The commander of the air base issued the orders to ban any appearance within his area of responsibility: the established perimeter line ran between the villages of Željava, Čelopek, k.377 or Abdića Brdo, to Klokot. As Colonel Milan Menićanin stated during a TV interview in March 1992, 'Since 1 April [1991] the high combat readiness was introduced. The units were on maximal alert'.[1]

According to an order issued by the HQ RV i PVO on 9 May 1991, all of the firing positions along the perimeter were revitalised, all of the available artillery pieces were maintained in full operational status at all times of the day, and spare ammunition was stocked nearby. The same order specified that any attacks on the members of the units or their families should be countered by the use of available firearms. Finally, it warned that no identification symbols were permitted to be worn other than those approved by the regulations of the Yugoslav armed forces.

In this early stage of the growing conflict, all the reservists of 200th Light Air Defence Artillery Regiment and 200th Infantry Company were mobilised. The personnel were activated to serve with a call to take part in an exercise rather than war. They were rotated in shifts of 15 days, and sent back home after each shift, taking their uniform and equipment with them – but without their firearms.[2]

Armed with UB-16 unguided rocket pods, MiG-21Bis K, No17203 of No. 125 Squadron, taxies out to the runways in early 1991. This particular aircraft was lost later in the year in a crash landing on 21 August, killing pilot Captain S. Ciglić. (via B. Pejić)

A line of the different versions of the MiG-21s belonging to 117th Regiment in 1990-91. (Author's collection)

War in Slovenia: Acting Safe Heaven for Cerklje AB

Ironically, the reservists were all sent back home by the time the short but sharp war in Slovenia erupted on 26 June 1991. This conflict thus caught 200th Air Base staffed only by its peace-time 'ready' force. To strengthen the reconnaissance capacity at Bihać, on 29 June a flight of No. 354 Reconnaissance Squadron from Ladjevci air base with five IJ-21 Jastrebs arrived and took part in the missions over Slovenia. At 23:00 on the same day RV i PVO HQ decided that Zagreb-Pleso based No. 679 Transport Squadron would be

Pilot Goran Mandić waits for another flight while MiG-21 Bis No. 17103 was prepared to take-off. Mandić would be shot down by Croatian forces in September 1991 and captured. (M. Popović)

MiG-21s from No. 124 and No. 125 squadrons took an active part in the small war in Slovenia from 26 June to 3 July 1991. Here, a MiG armed with Munja unguided rocket launchers is being parked back on the apron in autumn 1991. (Zoran Milovanović)

transferred to Batajnica, and part of them to Bihać. When arriving at Bihać, pilot Vladimir Rajtar, who later defected to the Croatian side, met the large crowd of the pilots evacuated from Cerklje. Most of them were Slovenes, or from other nationalities who had settled in Slovenia and raised families there; "...those unshaven, desperate faces I will never forget. All of them left wives and children in Slovenia, which now they should to bomb. Many Croats openly complained."[3]

When the Slovenian Territorial Defence forces opened fire with mortars on Cerklje air base on the afternoon of 27 June 1991, 82nd Aviation Brigade was ordered to take off and fly into safety. Once over the neighbouring Pleso-Zagreb air base, they continued on to Bihać the same afternoon. On the morning of 28 June, there were seven IJ-22 Oraos and a single IJ-21 Jastreb from No. 351 Reconnaissance Squadron, and a group of pilots and technicians from No. 238 Fighter-bomber Squadron. On the 3 July, all of the Orao and Jastreb strike aircraft from Nos. 237 and 238 squadrons were gathered in Bihać. But, due to a total collapse of morale among personnel, this was not a combat unit anymore and most of them decided to abandon the RV i PVO and return to Slovenia or to join the emerging Croatian forces.

The remaining personnel of No. 351 Reconnaissance Squadron joined No. 352 Reconnaissance Squadron as a detachment and continued to operate with their IJ-21 Jastrebs. This unit was stationed at Runway No. 5. The remaining fleet of the 82nd Aviation Brigade was gathered at Udbina air base and remained there until 11 August. They were then transferred to Banja Luka Air Base, reorganised into No. 238 FB Squadron and joined 117th Fighter Regiment. After the settlement of the former Cerklje 474th Air Base in Banja Luka, 200th Air Base turned the maintenance and the logistics of No. 238 Squadron over to this unit. Twenty days later, 117th Fighter Regiment was reorganised into 117th Aviation Brigade which had previously included Nos. 124, 125 and 352 squadrons. The HQ Detachment and

MiG-21Bis No. 17103 piloted by Captain Dronjak, belonging to No. 124 Squadron, suffered a crash landing on 26 April 1991 after running into holes alongside the runway. (Branislav Dronjak)

No. 238 FB Squadron from the former 82nd Aviation Brigade and No. 129 Fighter Squadron based in Pula would also join when they abandoned their air base after 30 October.

Since the beginning of the conflict in Slovenia, and later in Croatia, Mi-8 and Gazelle helicopters of 111th Aviation Brigade based at Zagreb-Pleso were present at Bihać AB. They were used in numerous liaison, transport and SAR missions. Some of the Gazelles belonged to Fifth Military District which was in the Slunj area during the autumn. During this period, Menićanin, the commander of 200th Air Base had a single Gazelle attached permanently from Zagreb piloted by Duško Stanivuković and used the call-sign "Fox."[4]

The clash in Slovenia was brought to an end on 7 July 1991, when in accordance with an agreement with ministers of the EC a declaration

A group of four reconnaissance Jastrebs and two Galebs from the Cerklje based No. 351 Squadron joined 117th Aviation Brigade and continued to operate as an attachment to No. 352 Reconnaissance Squadron during the second half of 1991. (Z. Milovanović)

was signed at Brioni and a truce, the deployment of international monitors, a three month moratorium on the of secession of the republics Slovenia and Croatia, and a total withdrawal of the Yugoslav Army was agreed.[5]

Activation of Udbina Air Base

In this period, Udbina Forward Operations Base (FOB) was activated. To staff this, RV i PVO drew elements from 200th Air Base, and reinforced these with mobilised reservists, thus establishing the unit designated as 6th Battalion Operational Maintenance. Flying personnel were then provided by 82nd Aviation Brigade, the personnel of which arrived there just wearing their flying suits. Correspondingly, 200th Air Base was tasked with re-dressing, reequipping and accommodating them. 82nd Aviation Brigade remained at Udbina until early August 1991, when it was replaced by 240th Squadron from Mostar. Finally, in October 1991, 84th Air Base evacuated Zadar-Zemunik Air Base and moved to Udbina, finally relieving 200th Air Base of the responsibility for this FOB.[6]

A unique episode for 200th Air Base in 1991 was the introduction of a battalion with M36 Jackson Gun Motor Carriages. This type was first delivered to the JNA through the MDAP programme in first half of the 1950s. Highly reliable, they remained in service throughout the new war, and were usually deployed to equip self-propelled anti-tank battalions in the active and reserve infantry brigades, and one of the latter was based in Bihać. Its M36s were last overhauled in 1988-1989, but in 1991 a decision was taken to send them to Slovenia, where they were to be spent as targets at an army range south of Postojna. The ill-fated tank destroyers were already loaded on a train when the commander of the reserve brigade, Captain (or Major) Oroz contacted Colonel Menićanin with a request to prevent their destruction. Menićanin then acted on his own: together with some of Oroz's men, he unloaded all 18 M36s and returned them to their base. Once there, in the course of a short meeting with all of the available officers, the decision was taken to organise them into three batteries and deploy two for the defence of the air base, while the third was sent to Udbina. The M36s continued

Bihać's MiGs and Cerklje's Jastrebs on the apron in autumn 1991. (Z. Milovanović)

One of the former Cerklje-based No. 351 Squadron's Orao IJ-22s, with a reconnaissance pod, returns to Bihać from a sortie in November 1991. (Milorad D. Ristić)

Two pilots along with ground crew of the Cerklje-based No. 351 Reconnaissance Squadron posing in front of Orao IJ-22 No. 25712 after a sortie. Bihać, November 1991. (M.D. Ristić)

SA-341/342 Gazelle liaison helicopters were used widely from Bihać air base. They had withdrawn from Pleso-Zagreb air base and were used to support the HQ of Fifth Military District at Slunj as well as V Air Corps and 200th Air Base at Bihać. (Author's collection)

Defence of Udbina base was initially given to 200th Light AD Artillery regiment which oparated self-propelled twin-30mm guns known as "Praga." (M.D. Ristić)

Improvised air traffic control, the so-called "Canadian Girl" at the Udbina FOB, which was initially subordinated to 200th Air Base, as seen in November 1991. (M.D. Ristić)

protecting Bihać AB until the spring of 1992, when they were handed over to other ground forces, but, during that one year the 200th Air Base was the only unit of the RV i PVO ever to operate self-propelled tank destroyers.[7]

V Air Corps HQ to Bihać Air Base

Summer months of 1991 brought up new challenges to Bihać AB. Colonel Menićanin recalled,

> In July, the Drežnik-Vaganac-Slunj road was blocked. Radio beacons were switched off. That meant there would be no flying in IFR conditions – only in ideal weather. At the same time, we received the information that the forces from Croatia were deploying in that area, bringing with them cannons and mortars …[8]

The squadrons from Bihać-based 117th Brigade became active flying over Croatia, ranging all the way from the Hungarian border to the Adriatic coast, and the unit began flying combat operations through late October and early November 1991.[9] Meanwhile, the situation in Bihać began to deteriorate. On 27 August 1991, Nenad Ibrahimpašić of the newly-established Muslim Party of Democratic Action (DPA) was elected as the new major of a nearby town. One of his first public appearances in this function was a call for all the citizens to boycott the JNA. Tensions began to grow, but there were no armed provocations from the Bosniaks. On the contrary, throughout this period the primary security challenge remained the Croats. As the number of clashes between them and the Serbs began to increase, inevitably, the JNA and the RV i PVO were slowly dragged into the war.

During the afternoon of 15 September 1991, the staff of the HQ of V Air Corps – the parent command of 200th Air Base – managed to evacuate Zagreb and to reach Bihać AB. With most of the officers and ranks arriving only with the uniform they wore, once again it fell to the local supply troops to provide replacements. About a month later, a separate building was constructed astride the entrance to the Objekt to accommodate this HQ, now commanded by a former MiG-21-pilot, General Bajić.

Three days later, at 0730 hrs on 18 September 1991, the evacuation of 129th Fighter (Training) Squadron at Pula AB in Croatia was ordered. All 12 of its aircraft were transferred to Bihać either the same day, or a day later: they included six MiG-21PFM, five MiG-21UM, and a single Utva liaison aircraft. In their place, 117th Aviation Brigade re-deployed six of its MiG-21bis to Pula – together with pilots and

Two MiG-21Bis seeing here on runway No.3, equipped with UB-16 launcher pods, returning from a sortie in November 1991. (M.D. Ristić)

Bihać apron no. 3 at war, November 1991. No. 17229 armed with Munja unguided rocket launcher pods is prepared prior to sortie. (M.D. Ristić)

Bihać apron no. 3 at war, November 1991. Two MiG-21Bis, carrying Munja unguided rocket launcher pods are prepared. In front is a reconnaissance Orao IJ-22, no. 25712, just returned from a sortie. (M.D. Ristić)

Fortification works at Abdića Brdo/k.377 in November 1991. (M.D. Ristić)

ground personnel – to provide a further QRA and fly CAPs until all the JNA troops could be evacuated from the Istrian Peninsula in Croatia.[10] The MiGs from Pula – and their pilots – all cadets of the Air Force Academy – did not stay at Bihać for very long: only a few days later this unit was re-deployed to Tuzla in north-eastern Bosnia from where its fliers could operate in more favourable weather and with better ground support.

Under Mortar Fire

Soon after V Air Corps arrived at Bihać AB, it was followed by two other major commands from Zagreb. V Military District from Zagreb arrived at the firing range at Slunj and there established its HQ responsible for JNA's forces in central Croatia and western Bosnia. Moreover, X Corps JNA then evacuated Zagreb and settled within 27 July Barracks in Bihać. Several smaller units were located in Bihać, with the exception of 306th Light Air Defence Artillery Regiment, which was housed at Čelopek, within the perimeter of the air base.[11] Finally, control over all the local army units and the Serbian TO units was assumed by 6th Operational Group, the area of responsibility of which began at the fence of Bihać AB.[12]

Since 200th Air Base was the largest military unit in the wider area, and it operated a large number of transport vehicles, it was assigned the responsibility for the resettlement of all of these higher HQs. Moreover, 200th Air Base dispatched its personnel and vehicles for relocation of the stores and isolsated barracks surrounded by the Croatian forces. Mostly, the Bihać personnel were engaged in evacuation of the logistical base in Karlovac, with assets and stores in Skradnik, Jasenica and Sveti Rok. Most of the armament and material were passed to 6th Operational Group. The rest of the equipment – including over 100,000 items of firearms, ammunition of different

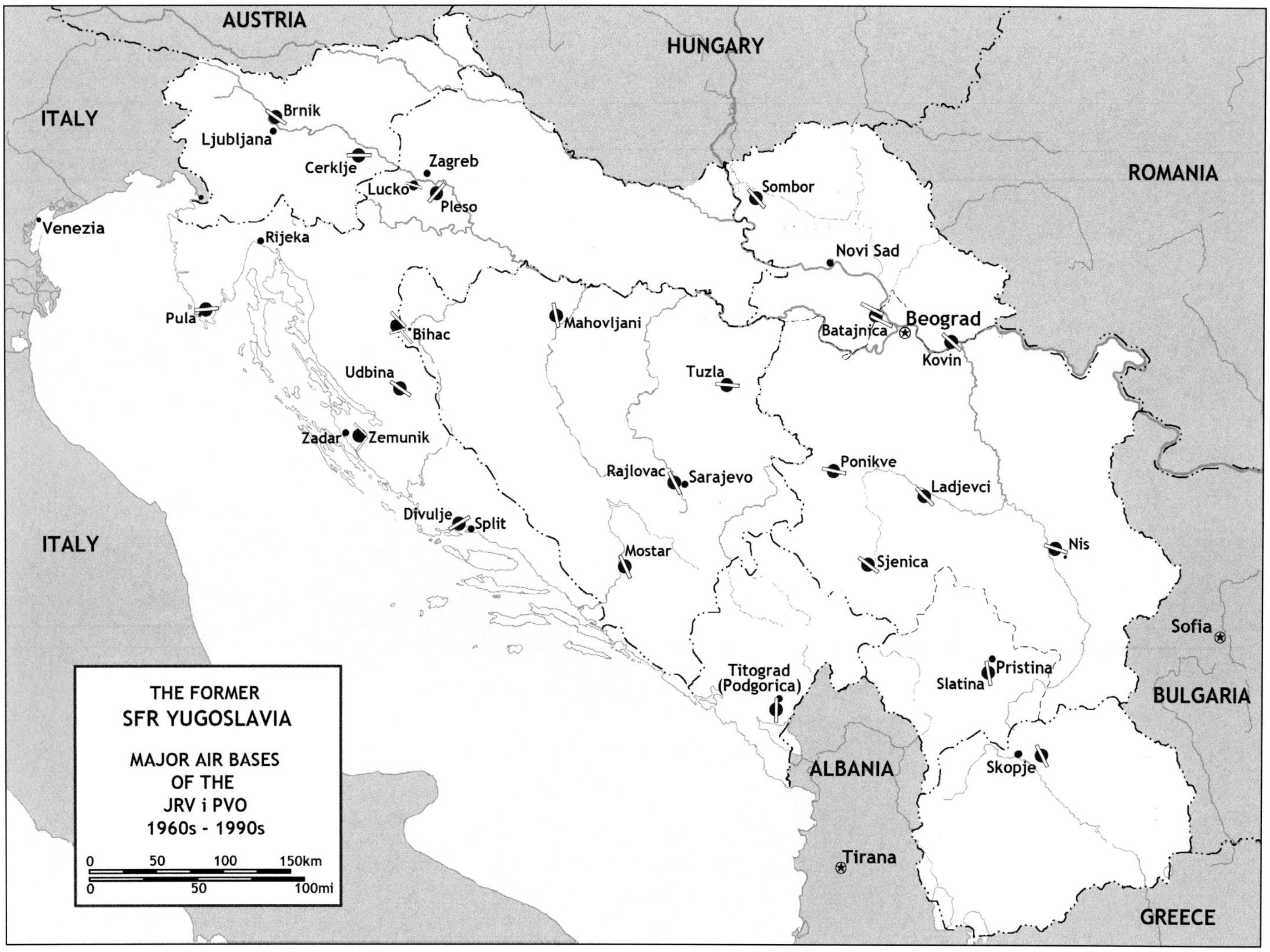

calibres, and significant quantities of fuel – were stored within the depots of 200th Air Base. Obviously, this was a massive burden for the personnel at Bihać AB, and before long the local storage facilities were hopelessly overstuffed. This resulted in equipment being spread all around the inside of the air base. On the other hand, the evacuation 'freed' a lots of air base personnel and vehicles to act as the main resettlement party. The movement of their convoys was always protected by the military police, who often also had to lend a hand in unloading the precious cargo. These demanding tasks removed a lot of air base personnel from their basic duty of enabling safe flying operations – which continued unabated during the same period.[13]

Colonel Menićanin has pointed out that the Croatian locals of Drežnik "were ordered to abandon the village and new inhabitants came... the Zbor Narodne Garde. Vaganac and Rakovica became ZNG strongholds with additional fortification of the houses. Everything was ready. And then, on a couple of occasions, shelling of the air base began".[14] The locations that Menićanin mentioned to the north-west of the air base, directly on the axis of the main runway.

The first mortar attack took place on 8 October 1991, when Croatian forces deployed in Vaganac – the village closest to Bihać AB – opened fire.[15] Knowing about the importance of the facility, the JNA commanders were not the least willing to tolerate this threat: correspondingly, 6th Operational Group deployed its Serbian Territorial Defence troops into an attack, which expelled the ZNG from Vaganac – together with most of its Croatian inhabitants. Twenty captured troops of the Croatian ZNG were sent to the Prisoner of War Camp in Manjača, while their 'collaborators' were sent to Croatia. Later on, the JNA moved on the village of Slunj and several others, further north-west, expelling Croatian troops – and the local population. With this, the problem of Croatian attacks was solved once and for all, and they never occurred again (at least not until the Croatian Army captured the destroyed Bihać AB in 1995).

However, the JNA and RV i PVO troops deployed at and around the base now began facing another problem: the local Serbian territorials began looting the emptied Croatian villages. Menićanin reacted by issuing the order for the looters to be stopped: a total of 18 were disarmed and arrested.[16] However, when Menićanin ran into another group of Serbian Territorial Defence troops in Vaganac, and attempted to stop a tractor loaded with looted goods, he was shot with an ancient Soviet PPSh-41 Shpagin submachine gun, and severely wounded.[17] Ironically, the commander of the most advanced and complex Yugoslav air base – one designed and constructed to survive a nuclear war – was thus wounded by an ancient weapon while wrestling with looters in a destroyed village at the edge of the base.

Atmosphere at Bihać Air Base

The sudden and very sharp war in Slovenia which continued on to Croatia brought about many unpredicted temptations for the personnel at Bihać Air Base. During the short war in Slovenia, some of the personnel began to hesitate, or refused orders to take part in the combat missions. Others slowly sided with the secessionist republics of Slovenia and Croatia. During July 1991 Slovenes abandoned the service. Next, a problem erupted with Croats and then the Muslim personnel and some conscript soldiers deserted. Divisions among the personnel in the air base were obvious: those pilots who did not want to carry out their orders were ordered to stop carrying their sidearms

The interior of Željava barracks, November 1991. (M.D. Ristić)

and or wear their pilot boots. Nevertheless, several pilots of Croatian origin continued flying and fighting for the RV i PVO – including some that would later defect with their MiG-21s to Croatia. Unsurprisingly, there was a great deal of mutual suspicion between the officers and other ranks, with nobody being sure who was on whose side.[18]

In addition to mutual suspicion, uncertainty about the future and the prospects for personal and family status and safety, occasional desertions, bitter discussions about Croatian and Serbian politics, request that all Croats and Muslims should be declared unreliable and separated – all resulted in severe psychological strain for everybody involved. Combat operations added their portion. As Captain Grandić recalled:

> In peace-time, our orders arrived over the telephone. Soon after it was discovered that the Croat National TV and radio stations were issuing public alerts whenever a MiG was taking-off from Bihać, it became obvious that 'unauthorised persons' were revealing sensitive information – including such as specific targets – to Zagreb. To avoid the use of tapped telephone lines, field telephones were used instead. To further improve the security, squadron COs began issuing orders to their pilots personally, and directly before the take-off.[19]

Years later, Croatian sources revealed that several officers and NCOs working in the communication units, and several civilians working at the post office in Bihać had provided 'valuable information' about the activities of 117th Aviation Brigade. The situation culminated on 25 October 1991, when Captain 1st Class Rudolf Perešin from the 352nd Squadron failed to return to from a reconnaissance mission over Slovenia: he actually decided not to fly back, but continued all the way to Klagenfurt, in Austria, landed there, and requested asylum. In reaction to this defection, General Bajić then ordered the arrest of the CO of No. 352 Squadron (a Serb), and his Security Officer (a Croat), while several suspected officers of Croatian nationality were removed from their posts.[20] Even then, the majority of the personnel of 117th Brigade continued serving: certainly enough, most of them were Serbs, but there were also Croats, Muslims, Macedonians, and Hungarians, and the CO of the unit was a Bosnian Muslim – all determined to defend Yugoslavia from separatists. As Predrag Grandić, later shot down by the Croatian armed forces bitterly concluded 'we were still Yugoslavs'.[21]

Bihać Air Base Supports Further Evacuations

At the conference held in The Hague in November 1991, an agreement was reached for the safe withdrawal of the remaining JNA forces from the Republic of Croatia. This, the so-called Vance Peace Plan, enabled a relatively peaceful evacuation of several besieged units of the RV i PVO – foremost the Zagreb-Pleso AB. On 30 November 1991, a column carrying the troops of 5th Air Surveillance Regiment moved out of Pleso bound for Bihać while monitored by the observers of the European Community (EC) and the Croatian Police. While passing down the motorway connecting Zagreb with Belgrade, they were verbally attacked by bystanders: nevertheless, their column reached Bihać safely, the same evening.

Unexpected guest: an Iraqi Air Force MiG-23ML that was ferried from "Zmaj" Air Depot, near Zagreb, to Bihać in December 1991. It remained in Bihać until February 1992. (M.D. Ristić)

General Ljubomir Bajić, commander of V Air Corps, with the mayor of Bihać Nenad Ibrahimpašić (in the middle) and the commanders, all lieutenant colonels, of the units stationed in the air base, right to left: Veselinović (111th Helicopter Regiment), Skadrak (117th Aviation Brigade), Kastratović (200th Light AD Artillery Regiment) and partly visible Menićanin (200th Air Base) Bihać. 22 December 1991. (B.Pejic)

The next issue was much more complex, and included the evacuation of the Zmaj Works – a major overhaul depot situated in Velika Gorica, south of Zagreb, which was working on over 20 MiG-21s and MiG 23s of the Iraqi Air Force when the war erupted. While nearly all the aircraft were in a disassembled condition, a single intact Iraqi MiG-23ML was flown by Major Omer Avdaković to Bihać AB, where it remained stored for several months afterwards. The reason was obvious: not only was Avdaković a veteran of 352nd Squadron with experience from operating from the local air base, but he had also converted to the MiG-23ML in Hungary, and worked as a test pilot at Zmaj. Once in Bihać, the Iraqi national markings on the jet were overpainted by the Yugoslav national insignia. Following several minor repairs, the aircraft was then flown to Batajnica AB, outside Belgrade, in January 1992.[22]

On 30 November, 117th Aviation Brigade at the Bihać operated total of 47 MiG-21 of seven different sub-versions (PFM, R, MF, Bis/Bis-K, U, US and UM). They used the standard and proven repertoire of ordnance: FAB, PLAB, BL-755 bombs and 57mm and 128mm unguided rockets.[23]

A crew with the evacuated Marconi S-600 of the 5th Air Surveillance Regiment at Abdića Brdo k.377. (M.D. Ristić)

As some kind of replacement or back-up for the Bihać squadrons, 130th Fighter Squadron was sent from Priština to Bihać and landed on 19 November with ten MiG-21Ms and one two-seater. 130th Squadron mostly carried out QRA, CAP and escort missions over the Yugoslav Army units which were withdrawn from their surrounded garrisons in Croatia. After 27 days spent in Bihać, 130th Squadron returned to its home-base at Priština on 26 December 1991.[24]

As the situation started to become more complicated, the entire defensive belt on the inner side of the perimeter fence, covering some 15 kilometres, was mined. During the winter of 1991/92, it was noted that children from the neighbouring Muslim village of Izačić were entering the minefield and removing the mines. This, perhaps inevitably, had a tragic outcome. Having removed a number of mines and taken these with them three boys stopped near a fire in Vedro Polje to warm up. The mines exploded and the boys were killed. Their funeral raised extreme tensions in the village, were the inhabitants protested against the army and the practice of setting minefields.

The shuttle coach (TAM) from 51st Air Surveillance Battalion HQ in Željava seen here on the mountain lane that led to the radar position at Gola Plješevica, November 1991. (M.D. Ristić)

A shift at Gola Plješevica works in the "Furnus" cab of the Marconi S-600 radar, November 1991. (M.D. Ristić)

Suddenly, the local imam made a speech where he explained how the boys were killed and rejected the bitter accusations made against the army. Colonel Menićanin concluded that he was grateful to the imam for such reasonable behaviour, and thanks to this gesture there were no related security problems while the air base remained. Furthermore, some of the villagers who worked in Western Europe were evacuated aboard RV i PVO transport aircraft, together with personnel of the air base, in April and May 1992.[25]

Despite the expanding conflict, the situation in the city of Bihać had remained more or less unchanged. The strength of the garrison was now reinforced with many units and HQs that had arrived from Croatia and this was an important factor. The size of the military population in the city, mixed marriages and the cautious approach of the local authorities resulted in no rise of tensions. In the same period however, the Air Force authorities noted "Croatian propaganda" and disturbing telephone calls to the senior officers of the air base, though in most cases, the callers who cursed and threatened remained unknown. Slowly the effects from the war in neighbouring Croatia started to grow, as did the black market. Serious negative influences started to come from Cazinska Krajina, a densely populated Muslim area north of Bihać.

The next step was a change in the local Bihać police. With the appointment of the new chief of the Public Security Centre known by the nick name "Landi", relations between the local police and members of the Army and Air Force became much more belligerent. During early 1992 the situation in Bihać started to become serious due to the rise in tensions over Bosnia and Herzegovina. Threats to army personnel and their families became frequent. There were various comments that they were "chetniks" or "communists", depending on the situation.[26]

To match the information gap at Bihać Air Base, the garrison, and the city itself, in late December a magazine titled *Orlovi Plješevice* (*The Eagles of Plješevica*) was launched. There were a total of eight issues of this war-time magazine, which was edited by the Press Centre established in the Army Club in downtown Bihać. Headed by Lieutenant Colonel Dušan Knežević, this magazine was an example of how the military authorities tried to cope with the rising threat of war which surrounded the air base day by day.[27]

51st Air Surveillance Battalion in 1991

On 25 June 1991, the 51st Air Surveillance Battalion was raised to a high level of readiness alongside other air surveillance units. In this period its P-35 and PRV-11 radars at Abdića Brdo were dismounted and set up in "marching" position.

On 7 July 1991 the AN/TPS-63 radar was transferred from 5th Battalion HQ at Kurilovec to Plješevica and was used until the S-600 radar was overhauled. On 13 August the modern AN/TPS-70 radar was moved from Abdića Brdo to the Belgrade-based 1st Air Surveillance Regiment. When the overhauling of the S-600 radar at Plješevica was finished the AN/TPS 63 was moved from Plješevica down to the Abdića Brdo site on 24 August.

After the short war in Slovenia, 1st Company of the 91st Battalion, 5th Air Surveillance Regiment, from Ljubljanski Vrh were ordered to move to Bihać/Plješevica, on 18 and 24 August 1991. This movement enabled the arctic radome at Plješevica to be replaced with the one which arrived from Ljubljana. The S-600 radar also remained on the site and on 23 September was introduced into the working shifts. When the Plješevica site was stabilised with radars and dome, it was decided that the AN/TPS-63 from Abdića Brdo should be moved to Kozara mountain near Banja Luka.

On 10 July 1991 a new AS-84 automated system built with Marconi hardware elements was brought to Objekt Klek. Work to accommodate the AS-84 in the Objekt started immediately. The system started to work at full capacity on 15 September 1991, on the day when the HQ of 5th Air Corps arrived at Bihać and established its "reserve" command post.

On 21 September, during the clashes in Croatia, personnel from the 1st (independent, long range) Radar Company near Sisak were evacuated to Bihać aboard two Mi-8 helicopters. The HQ of 5th Air Surveillance Regiment at Pleso-Zagreb air base were trapped, with an AS-84 system and other radar equipment, for a further two months. After the agreement was reached between Yugoslav Army and Croatian authorities a safe passage to Bihać was agreed. The column

Celebration of Army Day on 22 December 1991 at Bihać Air Base. Lt Colonel Skadrak decorates notable members of 117th Brigade, while General Bajić (in the camouflaged uniform) and Lt Colonel Menićanin stand aside. In the rear, a QRA pair and an APA (APU) vehicle are visible. The MiGs' canopies are covered and appear to be at a low degree of combat readiness. (M.D. Ristić)

Two MiG-21Bis being fuelled after a sortie in 1990-91. In front is No. 17133 which became the first Croatian Air Force MiG-21 when pilot Borović defected on 4 February 1992. The other one, No. 17130 was shot down in December 1991, but pilot Roberto della Crocce ejected safely. (Istok Micić)

MiG-21 Bis No. 17211 was damaged during a combat sortie and was used as a test bed near apron no. 3. (M.D. Ristić)

from Bihać moved on 24 November but it was halted and partly captured by Croatian forces on following day despite the agreement. The column reached Pleso on the night of 26 November and joined the evacuation of 5th Regiment's HQ. The column of 62 military and 25 private vehicles arrived in Bihać on the afternoon of 30 November.[28]

5

Final Days of Bihać Air Base and Beyond

Spring of 1992 – the end of Bihać Air Base

After the truce in Croatia was signed on 2 January 1992, clashes between the Yugoslav Army and local Serbian Krajina forces on one side and Croatian forces on the other side ceased. A total cease-fire started on 3 January 1992 at 18:00. It was agreed that a UN peace-keeping force should enter the conflict zones and divide the fractions. The RV i PVO halted its combat activities.

The truce in January 1992 brought about a long awaited break, but it did not lead to a solution or any improvement in the political situation. The shadow of war remained over the whole area.

The air base and aviation brigade attempted to continue with their peacetime tasks: maintenance, training and QRA. Some of the personnel took leave. After pilot Danijel Borović deserted to the Croatian side during a regular sortie on 4 February, tensions and suspicions among the personnel rose again. Gatherings and meetings with 5th Air Corps commander General Bajić on 5 February, and RV i PVO commander General Stefanović on 4 March, did not help or resolve numerous questions, objections and comments raised by angry pilots and other personnel. Such a situation produced further deterioration of moralc among the pilots. Many started to primarily take care of themselves and their families in the city of Bihać that was no longer secure for military personnel and their next of kin.[1]

What is obvious from these statistics is that three of the squadrons at Bihać retained their squadron size by based on the number of the available aircraft. On the other hand pilots able to carry out missions were in the range of detachment or flight size. It was a sign that the combat readiness of the brigade was decling as the political situation started to get worse day by day.

The serious problem came in February 1992: the deployment of the UN peace-keeping forces. Bihać Air Base was at the edge of Bosnia and Herzegovina and Croatia. Within the Croatian side were the Serb populated areas which proclaimed themselves as the Republic of Srpska Krajina. As Croatia became independent the UN Security Council proclaimed the Krajina territory as a UN Protected Area, where UNPROFOR forces were later deployed. Arrival of the first UN monitors marked the start of the slow withdrawal of the federal forces. By the beginning of February, the UN monitors were settled in the Army Club in Bihać. Their deployment led to the restriction of flying from Bihać as flying was allowed to only the Bosnian side and was banned from flying over UNPA/Krajina (Croatian) territory. It led to the introduction of new procedures for taking off and landing, as well as carrying out daily missions.[2]

No matter the limitations, the Bihać MiGs continued to carry out regular air defence missions and even some exercises with 51st Air Surveillance Battalion during the February and March 1992. Even

Table 6: Aircraft and Pilots of 117th Aviation Brigade, early March 1992

Unit	Available aircraft	Air-worthy	Total number of pilots	Pilots capable for missions
No. 124	15	11	13	4
No. 125	17	14	16	8
No. 352	14 + 9 attached	12+7	14	5
No. 238 FB at Banja Luka	21	6	22	11
Total	76	60	65	28

The very last commander of 200th Air Base, Colonel Menićanin, gives an interview a few weeks prior to the evacuation of the base. (M. Menićanin)

more, just a couple of days prior to the escalation of the war in Bosnia and Herzegovina, it was ordered that only the QRA fighter pair would remain at the higher level of combat readiness.[3]

Those new circumstances were decisive for the future of Bihać Air Base. In the second half of March, Colonel Menićanin was summoned to RV i PVO HQ in Zemun. There he was informed that the air base would be abandoned and it was ordered that the underground Objekt should be mined and destroyed to prevent any further operational usage. Menićanin returned to his air base full of worries, the difficulties were yet to come, and his task was highly demanding.[4]

Early Clashes Around the Base

An explosion of clashes in many different areas of Bosnia and Herzegovina starting from 26-27 March were the first steps in the coming war. By the beginning of April, the squadrons from Bihać were active in different parts of Bosnia and Herzegovina and it was far from clear who was who on the ground. The exception was the advance of the Croatian regular forces in Posavina, middle-north Bosnia, and western Herzegovina. The MiGs from Bihać were engaged over those two front-lines, mostly conducting observation and reconnaissance sorties. Some demonstration sorties were carried out over Sarajevo to warn the local government against their attempts to abandon the already-broken Yugoslavia. The sorties over advancing Croatian forces mostly declined after 12 April when Captain Grandić in his MiG-21R (No. 26111) was shot down over the Kupres highlands and captured. Reading the details in pilot log books, we can conclude that the last combat sorties carried out from Bihać were on 16 and 17 April 1992.

International recognition of Bosnia and Herzegovina on 6-7 April 1992 marked another important sign that the air base should be evacuated soon as possible. Those sudden changes brought about a definitive change of attitude from the local Bihać authorities to the Air Base HQ. In the city there were the regular civil authorities and the newly established "war-time" authorities. One delegation headed by the president of the community in Bihać and chief of the Public Security Centre paid a sudden visit to the Air Base commander Colonel Menićanin and asked him to surrender the air base to the local authorities in Bihać. Menićanin listened carefully to the request from the people he used to work with, and sometimes to celebrate different occasions with, but refused any further talks on this question.[5]

In the following days, the Bosnia and Herzegovina Territorial Defence (TO BiH) forces started to spring up across the whole district of Bihać. On 7 April, the Special Purpose detachment was created in Bihać. Two days later, in the vicinity of Cazin, the 101st Independent Muslim Krajina Brigade was formed. By 20 April, Bosnia and Herzegovina TO forces were established in all of the Bihać district communities. The local police forces were in most cases the best organised and equipped men.[6] The TO BiH forces were light infantry units but with clear attitude not to tolerate Yugoslav Army or Serb forces on "their" territories.

On 15 April the Air Base HQ was informed that ground forces would be deployed to strengthen its defence. The air base and garrison in Bihać were still strongholds that nobody from the BiH/Muslim side wanted to challenge. On the "Croatian" side, the vicinity of the air base was controlled by the UN, Serbian territorials and the Yugoslav

MiG-21Rs seen at Batajnica in May 1992, shortly after abandoning Bihać. (M. Micevski)

Army. On the other side, the air base was still not a threat for the Muslim communities, but, within Bihać Air Base there was a growing realisation that since the worsening of situation and rise of the TO BiH forces, the Muslim villages of Gate and Izačić, that overlooked the runways, could be used as a point of direct attack on the base.

The 21 April clashes between Muslims and Serbs that had started in Bosanska Krupa, Bosanski Petrovac and Cazin and continued in May. Soon after the clashes expanded the Federal Army started to be perceived as the enemy. On 1 May the Muslim Bihać District Territorial Defence HQ ordered to its local units and HQs to take up defensive positions against the federal forces in the whole Bihać district. The war around the air base was expanding day by day.

Evacuation of the 117th Aviation Brigade

As the situation in Bihać city and surrounding areas started to become more complicated, the number of sorties by 117th Brigade started to decline.[7] During this time, most of the Muslim personnel, mainly from the air technical service, decided to abandon the RV i PVO ranks. Among the personnel who remained in service, the worries for their families in the city grew. There was information on the creation of a new reduced Yugoslavia, but actually nobody knew what the outcome of the growing tensions in BiH and Bihać community would be.

On 21 April, a Gazelle helicopter which was flying from Banja Luka back to Bihać with deputy CO of 117th Aviation Brigade Lieutenant Colonel Kusturić on board was hit by fire from the ground but managed to land in the base. It seems that on this day it was officially announced to the personnel that the air base and its personnel would be evacuated. It was truly a shock for many of them. Roberto della Crocce wrote: "In the pilot classroom, after the order (for movement to Serbia) was announced, some of the pilots, stood up and said that they would not take part [in the transfer of aircraft to Serbia] and that [they] are abandoning the unit... tedious and heavy situation. Everything what was hidden and silent in earlier months now exploded. No matter, we went to carry [out] the [transfer] overflight."[8]

Now, almost nobody cared about carrying out the necessary regular or combat missions. Everybody started to prepare to abandon Bihać. Some of the airmen decided to stay or to abandon the RV i PVO.

On the afternoon of the same day as the announcement, the pilots from Batajnica's 204th Fighter Regiment arrived. They took over the QRA and all other combat activities from Bihać's flyers. Some of them were dispatched to assist in the flying of the MiG-21 fleet to Serbia.[9]

Evacuation started immediately. The three squadrons of 117th Aviation Brigade left Bihać in groups over three days: 22-24 April. The first to move was No. 352 Reconnaissance Squadron, which arrived at Batajnica during 22 and 23 April, and was placed under the command of 204th Aviation Brigade on the following day. The other two squadrons moved to the inactive Ponikve AB in south-western Serbia. After the arrival at those empty facilities No. 125 Squadron was disbanded. The remaining No. 124 Squadron was placed under the command of the Priština-based 83rd Regiment (which would later become an aviation brigade). After 48 years of continuous operations, 117th Aviation Brigade – one of the most elite RV i PVO units – thus ceased to exist.[10]

From 24 April, the commanders of 200th Air Base and what was left of 117th Aviation Brigade made lists of who was staying and who preferred to abandon the ranks of the Army. This choice meant, on one side, the demobilisation of those who did not want to go to Serbia, or an evacuation of the families and all their belongings for those who did want to go. There were many dilemmas about future status, even more so because the original order called for the entire base and the Objekt to be evacuated by 30 April 1992. However, this proved impossible and indeed, the evacuation continued well into mid-May.

The last members of 117th Aviation Brigade abandoned Bihać Air Base on 6 May 1992. They began their movement to Serbia, squeezed in 11 personal vehicles and mingled with the column of lorries and semitrailers with spare parts and other equipment. In the area of Prnjavor, they were stopped by the local Serb militia. After a long-lasting quarrel, the column was returned to Banja Luka air base, until safe passage was agreed. This final column of the 117th Brigade reached Serbia on the morning of 8 May 1992.[11]

However, some activity of the MiG-fighters from Bihać AB continued during these last days. On the morning of 25 April, a flight of MiG-21s from the Batajnica-based No. 126 Squadron arrived: they re-established the QRA fighter pair and prepared their jets for ground attack missions. The Batajnica pilots were replaced on 4 May by the flight that arrived from the Priština-based 83rd Fighter Regiment.

Finally, on 11 May 1992 at 12:30, the last group of MiGs from 83rd Regiment took off, carried out air strikes on targets in Posavina in northern Bosnia, and then flew over to Serbia. It was the last sortie by any MiG-designed fighters ever flown from Bihać Air Base.[12]

Mass Evacuation

The intensive activities for evacuation of 200th Air Base started to be carried out by late April. Due to the lack of the heavy transport vehicles the Air Base was forced to engage a large fleet of lorries from the local transport enterprises. It was a necessary step since the air base

Yugoslav Airlines DC-9s were pressed into service for the evacuation of civilians and troops from Bihać air base in April 1992. (MC Odbrana)

Povlačenje jugoslovenske vojske

Noć na pisti u iščekivanju aviona za evakuaciju iz Bosne, bez vode, hrane i predstave koliko će još puta morati da se povlače iz bivših jugoslovenskih republika, kao „okupatori"

Po travi oko stajanke bivalo je i po hiljadu vojnika koji osluškuju zvuk aviona iz pravca Beograda

Bosna nije Vijetnam

Danima je održavan vazdušni most sa bihaćkog vojnog aerodroma za odvoženje vojnika, civila i opreme, a onda je grandiozna eksplozija, 16. maja ujutro, označila neopozivi kraj jednog od najvažnijih vojnih objekata u Jugoslaviji, ali i same Jugoslavije kakva je u ovom veku bila

Piste broj 4 i 3, koje se završavaju pred ulazom u podzemne hangare, snimljene iz helikoptera

Početkom maja još su avioni, koji su sletali na vojni aerodrom „Željava" kraj Bihaća, bili puni paketa s lekovima, dečjom hranom i pelenama i još je u njima bilo više mesta za civile nego za ljude u uniformama. A onda-je, kako se bližila sredina meseca, sve manje civila stizalo avionima u ovu vojnu bazu, a sve je više bilo onih koji nisu uspevali da sa nje odu jer je vojska ubrzala svoju evakuaciju: obznanjeno je da do 19. maja, uprkos svim ranijim očekivanjima, Jugoslovenska armija ima da napusti teritoriju Bosne i Hercegovine, najnovije države na svetu, u bivšoj Jugoslaviji.

Na platou u podnožju Plješevice užurbanost je rasla. Nekada najčuvanija

INTERVJU, 29. MAJ 1992. 3

POVLAČENJE JUGOSLOVENSKE VOJSKE

da ga puste sa aerodroma samo na jedno pre podne, da iseli stvari iz Bihaća. Mesec i po nije stigao da ode do stana, a kad su ga pitali zar još veruje da nije obijen, odgovorio je: „Čulo bi se, miniran je sa više od dvadeset bombi". Sutradan se na aerodromu saznalo za epilog. Poručnik je dobio nekoliko slobodnih sati, spakovao pokućstvo u kamion i ispratio ga do izlaska iz Bihaća, ali su mu ubrzo javili da je na otvorenom putu kamion.

U petak uveče 15. maja na bihaćkom vojnom aerodromu gotovo nikoga više nije bilo. Poslednji vojni transporter „andonov" odleteo je još pre mraka, a poslednja kolona vojnih vozila izašla je prema Bihaću oko 22 časa. Te noći očekivalo se se da na aerodrom upadnu „zelene beretke", hosovci ili snage krajinske milicije jer su njihove grupe bile na svim stranama okolo.

U subotu ujutro, tačno u pet časova i 30 minuta odjeknula je snažna eksplozija na ulazu u aerodrom iz pravca Bihaća, u blizini strelišta. Tačno pet minuta pre šest časova začula se serija eksplozija na pistama i svih pet je prekrio dim. Eksplodirala su punjenja koja se inače ugrađuju na piste vojnih aerodroma po ivicama.

U 13 minuta pre osam časova i Bihać se zatresao od grandiozne eksplozije, a iz obronaka Plješevice suknuli su plamen i dim: uništena je podzemna instalacija gde su bili hangari, radionice, magacini i sve ostalo što je ovaj aerodrom činilo jednim od najvećih i najutvrđenijih u Evropi i zbog čega se njegova vrednost procenjivala na sumu između četiri i osam milijardi dolara. Ostala je čitava samo radarska stanica na vrhu Plješevice i administrativna granica između Hrvatske i Bosne, preko sredine nekadašnjeg aerodroma. □ S. Kačarević

Vojni aerodrom kod Bihaća viđen sa vrha Plješevice

Mladi vojnici su dočekali svoj avion koji će ih odneti sa bosanskog ratišta

Serija eksplozija i dim iznad piste: trenutak kada je aerodrom poleteo u vazduh

6 INTERVJU, 29. MAJ 1992.

Scenes from the evacuation of Bihać Air Base, April 1992, as seen in the Belgrade magazine *Intervju*. (*Intervju*)

had enormous amounts materiel, enlarged with evacuated materials, weaponry and equipment in autumn 1991. The large quantities of fuel especially were to be evacuated. Such quantities of almost everything complicated the evacuation. Finally there were the private possessions and furniture of the personnel who decided to leave Bihać.

The RV i PVO HQ ordered that the evacuation of Bihać Air Base should be the priority among other air bases in Bosnia and Herzegovina – Tuzla, Mostar and Rajlovac near Sarajevo – where the evacuation had also started. The air bridge was organised with standard AN-26 transports. The most valuable asset was a captured Uganda Cargo Boeing 707, which could ferry in one sortie several hundreds of cramped troops or civilians. The RV i PVO mobilised a few of the Yugoslav Airlines Boeing 727s and DC-9s, giving them military serials, and pressed them into the evacuation air-bridge. It was the practice that all transport planes arrived with a minimum of fuel, and at Bihać air base they were then filled to the maximum to use up the fuel in the air base.

To assist with the evacuation of the material goods members of 160th Air Technical Base from Pančevo arrived at Bihać and other air bases in Serbia also dispatched some of their personnel to assist the evacuation. Mi-8 and Gazelle helicopters from 111th Helicopter Regiment in Banja Luka were engaged to provide air cover to the convoy leaving Bihać and travelling through the Bosnian countryside where the first clashes had started. The evacuation was carried out in an organised fashion.

The air-bridge of RV i PVO transport aircraft was almost continuous. Ordnance had priority, though there were problems with the items packed in large boxes, such as the BL-755 Cluster bombs, AGM-65B Maverick AGMs, and various FAB, PLAB or other heavier bombs and as Colonel Menićanin recalls, there were 980 BL-755 cluster bombs evacuated. It was possible to load between 32 and 46 of such containers in a Boeing 707 and Menićanin borrowed a large forklift from somewhere in the city of Bihać to speed up this operation. The fuel was also a problem but it was mostly evacuated and what remained inside the Objekt's reservoirs was spoiled with some NBC powder. It was a kind of success in evacuation.[13]

In this period, the UN observers and initial parties from UNPROFOR arrived in Bihać. They provided some of their fuel for evacuation of the personnel of the garrison and each officer or NCO family was given single lorry. Two families shared a semitrailer. As Colonel Menićanin recalls, there were a total of 860 "military" families evacuated from Bihać organised in five or six large columns which headed to Serbia, avoiding the areas where the clashes had already started.[14]

Most of the members of 200th Air Base, and other units from Bihać, who were born in Serbia, Montenegro or other former republics of Yugoslavia left for Serbia. Others, that were of the Serbian nationality born in BiH moved to Banja Luka air base. Some left for Udbina where they joined Serb Krajina authorities.[15] Muslim personnel mostly remained in Bihać and later joined the TO/Army of BiH.

In the second half of April and the first days of May, the evacuation of materiel and equipment for the air base started. Columns of military and contracted lorries and semitrailers evacuated materiel out of the air base and its stores. As an illustration, on 5 May a column consisting of 18 semitrailers and other vehicles abandoned Bihać. They were stopped in Tuzla – by the local Muslim TO forces, but later allowed to continue to Serbia

"We were powerful until the last men went out", testifies the last CO of 200th Air Base, Colonel Menićanin.[16]

On 24 April the HQ of 5th Air Corps was disbanded. General Bajić and part of the HQ were evacuated from the air base to Serbia. The remaining personnel of this HQ, now as the 5th Operational Group, abandoned Bihać Air Base on 27 April and were transferred to Banja Luka. There they continued operating for the next twenty days with responsibility over the Air Force units in Banja Luka and evacuation parties in Bihać.[17]

After most of 200th Air Base was evacuated, the evacuation of other units also started: 200th Light Air Defence Regiment, 51st Air Surveillance Battalion and finally 379th Engineer Battalion.

Along with the air base, Bihać's 27 July and Grmeč barracks were also evacuated. Some of the effectives withdrew deeper into Serb-controlled territories. Most of the armaments that were kept in the air base's stores were left to the Serbian TO forces, along with the stores that were guarded by 200th Air Base around Bihać. The triple-barrelled M-55 20/3 mm AA guns belonging to the 200th Light AD Artillery Regiment were left to the Serb forces.[18] Some of the weapon and ammunition stores in the area of responsibility of 200th Air Base, such as in Svodna or Ripač, were turned over to TO BiH forces. Colonel Menićanin stated that the Muslim TO forces in Cazin and Kladuša were equipped with those weapons.[19]

200th Light AD Artillery Regiment prepared for the evacuation as had the other units. In the meantime most of the Muslim personnel and conscripts abandoned or deserted the unit. On 8 May the order "ready to march" was given. The Regiment withdrew its assets and formed a column during the night. In the morning of 9 May 200th Regiment started the march to Serbia along the route Bihać – Ključ – Banja Luka – Doboj – Tuzla – Bijeljina – Serbia. As noted the light 20/3 AA guns were left, but everything else from the AAA inventory remained with the column created from all remaining active, and part of the earlier mobilised reserve, personnel. The regiment spent the night at mines near Bosansko Petrovo Selo. Later on the next day, Serbian paramilitary forces halted the regiment in the area of the city of Bijeljina with the intention of disarming the unit and taking over their weaponry. Sidearms were drawn and, following tough negotiations between Colonel Kastratović and local para-military commanders, the regiment continued to Serbia reaching the air base at Ponikve, Western Serbia on the following day. There, sometime later the regiment was disbanded and became part of 165th Air Base.[20]

Moreover, by the beginning of May, Bihać Air Base became the main point of the aerial evacuation of Yugoslav Army troops that were leaving for Serbia. These were personnel and conscripts of the different ground forces units that were born out of the BiH and arrived at the air base where they waited for the aircraft which would evacuate them. They flocked around the runways and waited outside the Objekt. The air base provided them with meals and dry rations until they boarded the transport aircraft. Between the first week of May and 03:00 of 14 May, there were 3,520 evacuated, and another 725 were evacuated on that day.

Groups of civilians were also allowed into the air base. These were military families and civilians of Serb nationality who decided to abandon Bihać or Bosnia in general. Their personal vehicles were parked from both main entrances into the air base, from the Bihać and Željava side all the way to the runways. Family members carrying essential luggage waited in the parked cars or gathered on the grass between the runways. Even though evacuation continued without problems or panic, desperation was common among the civilians.

The moment of the explosions at the air base, early on the morning of 16 May as shown on a Sarajevo television broadcast. (Author's collection)

Under the order issued on 12 May 1992, 200th Air Base with its Light AD Artillery Regiment and 379th Engineer Battalion was to be transferred to Priština air base and to disband there, with all remaining personnel and equipment to join 492nd Air Base located there. Since most of the equipment had gone to other locations, and most of the personnel were scattered between Banja Luka, Udbina, Batajnica, Ponikve and elsewhere – and some of them had abandoned active service – this order was not carried out. 200th Air Base ceased to exist after the abandonment of Bihać.

During combat operations 200th Air Base lost three of its servicemen: a conscript soldier and NCO were killed by land mines in two separate accidents, and one member of the local TO detachment who was attached to defend the Air Base.[21]

According to later information from the Muslim Army of BiH, a total of 125 men belonging to the units at Bihać Air Base joined its ranks: 37 officers, 58 NCOs and 30 conscript soldiers.[22]

Destruction of the Underground Objekt

At the peak of the evacuation, on 10 May 1992, a transport aircraft arrived at Bihać AB with a motley group of airmen. It was a special team dispatched from RV i PVO HQ, consisting of several high-ranking officers and specialists from 333rd Engineer Battalion. Their task was to prepare the destruction of the underground Objekt and all of the runways. Some personnel of 200th Air Base and 379th Engineer Battalion were to assist them and their security detail was provided by paratroopers from 63rd Parachute Brigade, JNA.

How the air base looked on 15 May 1993 during the Bosnian War. (All photos by M.D. Ristić)

The approach to entrance C.

The demolished entrance C.

A view of the huts belonging to the QRA unit, fire-fighting unit with garage, a simulator room, classrooms and meteo-service, all on the left side of the taxiway which lead to entrance C.

Unrecognisable debris inside the demolished Objekt Klek.

One of the buildings on the left side of entrance C.

View from entrance C to former taxiway, leading to the "Triangle".

The team inspected the entire underground facility as well as the runways, in order to assess what kind of demolition was necessary and to inspect what was left to evacuate, before starting its actual work of mining the runways and Objekt Klek. The runways were mined first with a total of 27 tonnes of explosive placed at ten points. Because each of the runways had been constructed with such points for precisely such an eventuality, the technicians simply stuffed prepared holes with explosives and fuses.

Inside the Objekt, the team set explosives at most of the vital parts: the entrance doors, the air conditioning system, power-plant, heating system, elevators, ventilation and many other vital parts. A total of 50 tonnes of dynamite was used to destroy the Objekt: eight BL-755 cluster bombs which remained in the galleries were added to this destructive inventory.

The team constantly reported on the preparations and conditions in the Air Base to the Commander of the RV i PVO General Božidar Stefanović – former commander of 117th Regiment in the mid-1970s.[23] Meanwhile, the evacuation of the remaining personnel and all the useful equipment and items continued.

Early on the morning of 16 May 1992, at 05:53hrs local time, the sounding of a siren warned the population of Bihać of 'general danger'. Two minutes later, at exactly 05:55hrs, the first detonation took place: this destroyed the road leading from Bihać so as to warn anybody who might attempt to enter the base. The largest explosion, which destroyed the Objekt, occurred at 07:47hrs: it shook not just the base and its vicinity, but also the city of Bihać. 'The mountain boiled inside', as Colonel Menićanin recalled. The four entrances into galleries and five runways were destroyed or badly damaged by the explosions.

Radar position at Gola Plješevica, seen during the war in Bosnia 1992-1995, now part of the Vojska Republike Srpske. (Petko Rasević)

Prior to the first explosion, Three Mi-8s helicopters (Nos 12244, 12403 and 12405) and a locally modified reconnaissance SA.341 Gazelle 'Hera' (12709) arrived from Banja Luka AB to evacuate the demolition team. As the mines went off around the various positions, one by one the helicopters took off. The last to get airborne was the Hera with Colonel Menićanin and a cameraman who filmed the effects of the demolition: the colonel left his Steyr Puch command vehicle at the edge of the runway before boarding the helicopter.

Flying at extremely low level and avoiding larger settlements, all of the helicopters reached Zalužani helidrome outside Banja Luka. Amongst the landing gear of one of the Mi-8s were branches in which the ground crew discovered a small squirrel.

That was the end of Objekt Klek and Bihać Air Base as an organised facility of the RV i PVO.[24]

The entire demolition operation was considered a top-secret operation and thus kept secret even from the remaining personnel of 200th Air Base. During the morning and in reaction to the sound of explosions, two cars with personnel from the air base arrived at the gate on the Bihać side. They were halted by military police, who still guarded the perimeter, and redirected to the storage site in Ripač village, south from the town: seemingly, the 'less important' personnel were left behind, with sorely insufficient information about what to do once the Objekt was destroyed and their HQ abandoned.[25]

The media in Belgrade reported on the same day that 'thousands of Green Berets' – a Muslim paramilitary force – had overrun the base. Obviously, this was not true and it was actually the militia of Serbian Krajina (in Croatia) that appeared and took control of the demolished base's perimeter. Two days later, on 18 May 1992, the last 270 troops of the JNA left Bihać. Travelling in a column headed by the Chief of Staff of X Corps, Colonel Boric, and the town mayor (who agreed to secure a safe passage to the Serbian-controlled territories), they came away undisturbed. The Muslim-units of the TO BiH overran the 27 July and Grmeč barracks, following by the villages of Vedro Polje, Pokoj, and Orljani, a day later.[26]

The Last Outpost: Radar Station

While Bihać Air Base was thus rendered useless for all the warring parties, according to the video footage taken by the Armija BiH, by 1993 the north-western side, including the former radar site at Abdića Brdo/k.377 above Željava barracks to all of the entries to the Objekt were under the control of Serbian Krajina forces. The south-eastern part of the perimeter including the edge of the runway, base fence and former entrance from the direction of Bihać, was controlled by the Armija BiH. Most of the territory covering the former runways and taxiways was regarded as 'no-mans land'. Armed patrols from both sides were observing each other, but without serious attempts to seize the entire perimeter or the ruins of the air base.

The only asset of Bihać Air Base which remained operational was the radar site at Gola Plješevica. The HQ of its parent 51st Air Surveillance Battalion was evacuated from Bihać to Banja Luka on 11 May 1992. On the following day it became a unit of the newly established Army of the Serb Republic of BiH (VSR BiH, later VRS). On 13 May, 51st Air Surveillance Battalion renewed its air surveillance operations. No matter that Gola Plješevica remained on the Serb Krajina (now Croatian) side, this Radar Company was part of the Serbian Army in BiH through to the end of the war in 1995.

The radar company at Plješevica kept on working as the 1st Company of the 51st Air Surveillance Battalion with its British S-600 radars. In May 1992, it consisted of an S-654 radar in "full configuration": S-1020 large antennae of the surveillance radar, S-613 altimeter and S-5014B Furnus cab, all under the arctic cupola. The unit also had CD-2 automated system for purpose of civil air traffic control in Belgrade.[27]

After Bihać Air Base was abandoned, the company had only seven active officers and NCOs and ten reservist soldiers. The situation was peculiar and troublesome: there was nobody in the Air Base to provide support and provisions as had been done previously. The company was in the area of responsibility of Serb Krajina Militia, which literally did not care about their existence. Bihać garrison, had been taken over by the Muslim forces, which extended their control almost to the fences of the abandoned air base. The only protection was the minefield that provided security to the company, and the relative lack of interest of the Muslim forces to seize the radar site. It took several months before supply from the rest of the Serb Army in BiH should be established and the personnel of the radar company did not leave the site at Gola Plješevica for two months until mid-July of 1992! During this period the Serb light brigade in Ripač was tasked to take care on the radar company's logistical needs. Food was delivered when possible. The electric power only reached the site much later, in late October 1992, in the meantime the company operated only with generators to enable normal radar function.

This radar company at Plješevica was the most western Serb radar position and it kept operating for 24 hours per day. Since mid-1993, when NATO started to launch various air operations over Bosnia and Herzegovina, the site became a very important asset for Serb air surveillance and early warning. It enabled the Serbian Air force and Army to monitor all of the NATO activities in the air space of BiH. The Plješevica site also enabled the Serb Air Force and Serb forces in

Krajina to have up-to-date information on what was going on in the air as details of NATO or Croatian Ari Force activities were also sent to Serb Krajina HQ in Knin.

Prior to the NATO air attack on the Serbian-controlled Udbina Air Base, on 20 November 1994, the radar at Plješevica detected the approach of the attacking formations. Fearing that the site may be attacked by NATO, the commander of 1st Company was ordered to shut off its S-600 radar, leaving the other radar company at Kozara Mountain to track the attack formations further on. It was the first occasion that Serbian radar operators tracked and monitored a large scale NATO air attack.

1st Radar Company continued its work throughout 1995 monitoring and providing the information on NATO and Croatian air forces' activities. During this period the supplies for Plješevica were delivered by Serb Krajina Air Force helicopters, since the Serb forces had been pushed from the city of Bihać, and the supply line with Ripač ceased to exist. Muslim Armija BiH forces managed to fire several Malyutka ATGMs at the radar cupola causing damage to it and slightly damaging the radar antennae. Though it was repaired this was the first time that Plješevica radar site stopped working for 24 hours. It was a warning sign that the situation may deteriorate if an offensive should be carried out by any side against the mountain – as happened three months later.

Once the Croatian Army launched its large scale Operation Oluja (Storm) to regain control over the Serbian Krajina, on 4 August 1995, the Plješevica Radar Company was in serious trouble. The forces of the Serb Krajina were quickly defeated and Mount Plješevica surrounded from two sides. At the time, 207 officers and other ranks of 1st Radar Company and an infantry company providing security were deployed inside the mountain perimeter. The commander of 51st Aerial Surveillance Battalion promptly requested an evacuation, but initially, this request was turned down by top commanders in Belgrade. As the situation continued to deteriorate, the site was mined, and explosives installed on the radar antenna and all other important pieces of equipment. Finally, Belgrade gave in, the personnel were evacuated, and the site demolished during the evening of 5 August 1995: the troops marched down the mountain carrying the most important parts of the S-600 radar and its automated systems. After trekking about a dozen kilometres, they were picked up by a column of Serbian military vehicles at the Kamensko Saddle and then transported deeper into Serbian-controlled territory.[28]

A day later, advancing from the direction of Bihać, the forces of the Armija BiH reached the demolished radar station. A few hours later, the Croatian forces – slowed down by deep snow – followed up from their side, thus marking the end of the last remaining active facility of the once mighty Bihać, Tito's underground air base.

Bibliography

Archives

Hrvatski Državni Arhiv, Zagreb, Hrvatska, (Croatian State Archive, Zagreb, Croatia) fund: HR HDA 1211, 5. vojna oblast

Muzej Ratnog Vazduhoplovstva, Beograd, Srbija (Yugoslav Air Force Museum, Belgrade Airport, Serbia), fund: jedinice RV i PVO (The Units of the RV i PVO)

Muzej Jugoslavije, Beograd, Srbija (Museum of Yugoslavia, Belgrade, Serbia) fund: photo collection.

Vojni Arhiv Beograd, Srbija (Military Archive Belgrade, Serbia), fund: JNA (Yugoslav People's Army)

Newspapers and Magazines

Borba, Front, Intervju, Krila armije, Narodna armija, Orlovi Pljesevice, Politika,

Selected Bibliography

Bošković, Rajica. *Nebo na dlanu, Vek vazdusnog osmatranja, javljanja i navodjenja* (Belgrade: Author's Edition, 2017)

Della Croce, Roberto. *Priča jednog borbenog pilota* (Novi Sad: Stylos Art, 2013)

Dimitrijević, Bojan and Micevski, Milan. *117. lovački puk, 352. izviđačka avijacijska eskadrila, 200. vazduhoplovna baza* (Belgrade-Niš: Galaksija, 2015)

Dimitrijević, Bojan. *Izviđači Jugoslovenskog ratnog vazduhoplovstva* (Belgrade: Odbrana, 2011)

Dimitrijević, Bojan. *Jugoslovensko ratNo. vazduhoplovstvo 1942-1992* (Beograde: ISI, 2006)

Dimitrijević, Bojan. *Vazdušni rat nad Republikom Srpskom i Republikom Srpskom Krajinom* (Belgrade: Drustvo istoricara Srbije, 2017)

Felić, Bejdo Brigadir. *Peti korpus 1992-1995* (Sarajevo: Ljiljan, 2002)

Hamzić, Suad. *Letačke priče,* (Beograde: Tango Six Publishing, 2017)

Janša, Janez. *Premiki, Nastajanje in obramba slovenske države 1988–1992* (Ljubljana: Mladinska Knjiga, 1992).

Kronologija rata, Hrvatska 1989–1998 (Zagreb: Hrvatski Informativni Centar, 1998)

Micevski, Milan, and Dimitrijević, Bojan. *83.lovački puk* (Niš: Galaksija, 2016)

Micevski, Milan, and Dimitrijević, Bojan. Priča o 117. lovačkom puku - Gardijski lovci, *Aeroplan* (1, 1991)

Oluić, Sasa., Antić, Goran., and Dimitrijević, Bojan. *204.lovački avijacijski puk* (Belgrade: VINC, 2005)

Predojević, Dr Vaso. *U prodcjepu* (Belgrade: DanGraf, 1997)

Primorac, Branka. *Perešin, Život i smrt. O Rudolfu, ne samo pilotu...* .(Cakovec: Zrinski, 2001)

Radić, Aleksandar. 'Avion MiG-23 sa našim oznakama, Ratom oblikovana sudbina', *Arsenal* (special issue, Odbrana Magazine, No. 57, 1 September 2010)

Rajtar, Vladimir. *Nebeski ratnici, uspomene hrvatskog pilota* (Zagreb: Author's publication, 1995)

Razvoj oružanih snaga SFRJ 1945–1985, volume 4: *Ratno vazduhoplovstvo i protivvazdušna odrbana,* (Belgrade, VIZ, 1986)

DVD:

Tajne Željave, Vojni Aerodrom Željava kod Bihaća, 2009.

Web page:

http://Željava-lybi.com/forum,

Interviews with:

Milan Menićanin, Steva Miletić, Luka Kastratović, Dusan Buban, Branislav Dronjak, Predrag Grandić, Ranko Kovačević, Ranko Krivokapić, Rajko Lukić, Borislav Pejić, Milan Tepšić and Milan Milinković.

Notes

Introduction

1 While based on the border between the former Socialist Republic of Croatia and the former Socialist Republic of Bosnia and Herzegovina – two constituent federal states of the SFRJ – during the existence of Yugoslavia from 1945 until 1990, such boundaries were foremost regarded as civilian administrative borders between neighbouring communities. The Yugoslav National Army (Jugoslovenska Narodna Armija, JNA) and the JRV i PVO never especially paid much attention about such borders.

2 Since the end of the wars in the former Yugoslavia, in 1995, the former Bihać Air Base became a place of pilgrimage for many aviation and military enthusiasts. Since most of them have approached this huge, yet nowadays completely ruined complex from Croatia, and via the village of Zeljava, this name is widely used in the social media in particular. However, such a designation is completely inaccurate, and was never used while Bihać Air Base was in active service – regardless how much of its major complex was constructed near Zeljava. Indeed, in the parlance and in the official documentation of the JNA and the JRV i PVO, 'Zeljava' was the designation for a separate military facility, not related to Bihać Air Base. Instead, the JRV i PVO used either 'Bihać Air Base/Aerodrome', 'Objekt', 'Objekt Klek', or 'podzemni objekt' (underground object). Correspondingly, the same terminology is used throughout this volume.

3 In the former SFRJ, Pristina used to be the capitol of the Serbian autonomous province of Kosovo i Metohija. Since the war between NATO and Serbia of 1999, it is the capitol of the Republic Kosovo: a state widely recognised in the West, but neither by the Republic of Serbia nor the Russian Federation. Indeed, until today even the United Kingdom and the Kingdom of Spain have not officially recognised Kosovo as a sovereign, independent country.

Chapter 1

1 Muzej Jugoslovenskog ratnog vazduhoplovstva (MRV): fund RV i PVO: 'Istorija RV i PVO za 1962. godinu', p.48.

2 *Imenik podzemnih objekata*, Knjiga I, pp.6-20.

3 Podzemni vojni aerodrom Željava kod Bihaća – jedan od mitova SFRJ, https://www.gradjevinarstvo.rs /tekstovi/1454/820/podzemni-vojni-aerodrom-zeljava-kod-bihaca-jedan-od-mitova-sfrj (accessed 20 December 2014)

4 Vojni arhiv (VA): fund JNA: k. 20, f-2, d.3. 'Izveštaj o borbenoj gotovosti Ratnog vazduhoplovstva za 1956.god.'

5 *Imenik podzemnih objekata*, Knjiga I, pp.6-21.

6 Contrary to urban legends that emerged since the wars in former Yugoslavia, all villages had a mixed population of Serbs, Bosnian Muslims, and Croats.

7 MRV: k.27, 'Istorija 5. VaK, 1964-1972', appendix 14.

8 III uprava GŠ JNA, str. pov nar. 215, 12 May 1964. Notably, a unit with the same designation existed before: it was formed in March 1953 at Zalužani airfield north of Banja Luka. It was marked as "second category air base" responsible for training units. When they were disbanded, by early 1956, 200th Air Base ceased to exist and it was relegated to the 'R' status (a reserve unit, intended to be activated only in the event of a war), as a part of 151st Air Base at Pleso, outside Zagreb. In 1961, 200th 'R' Air Base was a 'paper formation' assigned to 399th Air Base in Tuzla. For details, see Dimitrijević, *Jugoslovensko ratNo. vazduhoplovstvo 1942-1992*, (ISI, Belgrade 2006). p.415.

9 VA: JNA: svežanj 3442-1973, p.4.

10 Podzemni vojni aerodrom Željava kod Bihaća – jedan od mitova SFRJ.

11 VA: JNA: k.164, f.2.11/2 'Naredba VK OS s.pov 11, 12 V 1958.' This unit was became an Engineer (Heavy) Regiment in 1959, but downsized to company in 1964. III uprava GŠ JNA, str. pov nar. 215, 8 June 1964.

12 MRV: Gradjevinska sluzba, 'Pregled izgradnje krupnijih objkekata u vezi inzinjerijskog uredjenja teritorije RV i PVO u 1969 godini'.

13 MRV: 'Istorija RV i PVO za 1962 godinu', p.48

14 In this context "Enterprise" refers to a civilian company though not, of course, a private one.

15 MRV: k.27, 'Istorija 5. VaK, 1964-1972', p.24.

16 VA: JNA: svežanj 3442-1973, 'Komanda RV i PVO, izveštaj o borbenoj gotovosti 1964' appendix: 'Aerodrom Bihać, I faza izgradnje'.

17 MRV: k.112, 'Formiranje i preformiranje jedinica u 1968', p.17; MRV: k.112, 'Formiranje i preformiranje jedinica u 1969 godini', pp.14-16.

18 MRV: k. 27, 'Istorija 5. VaK, 1964-1972', p.25; MRV: 'Istorija RV i PVO za 1965 godinu,' p.15. The unit was referred to as a "Range" as in "shooting range" and was the size of a small battalion.

19 VA: JNA: 3442-1973, 'Aerodrom Bihać, I faza izgradnje'.

20 MRV: k.112, 'Formiranje i preformiranje jedinica u 1968', p.17; MRV: k.112, 'Formiranje i preformiranje jedinica u 1969 godini', pp.14-16.

21 MRV: k.27, 'Istorija 5. VaK, 1964-1972', p.25; MRV: 'Istorija RV i PVO za 1965 godinu,' p.15.

22 Podzemni vojni aerodrom Željava kod Bihaća – jedan od mitova SFRJ.

23 MRV: k.27, 'Istorija 5. VaK, 1964-1972', p.143.

24 MRV: k.27, 'Istorija 5. VaK, 1964-1972', p.145.

25 National Photohgraphic Interpretation Center, 17 June 1968 (Approved for Release 2009/05/13: CIA-RDP 78t05929A003100040003-0, pp.2-4.

26 Suad Hamzić, *Letačke priče*, (Tango six, Belgrade 2017), p.86.

27 Komanda 5. puka VOJIN, str. pov. 25-187, 5.12.1975 [all documents of the 5.puk VOJIN/5th Air Surveillance Regiment courtesy by Colonel (ret.) Rajica Bošković].

Chapter 2

1 Hamzić, *Letačke priče*, p.87. An aviation regiment of the JRV i PVO included two or three squadrons, all operating the same type of aircraft. Furthermore, it consisted of a technical maintenance unit providing the so-called 1st (squadron) and 2nd (regimental) level of maintenance support. All other maintenance and logistics were provided by the home-base, which was a joint unit responsible for maintaining the aircraft, and provided maintenance to locally based units, air base security, and air defence, housing, and administrative issues. In peacetime, every air base operated just one airfield, but the aircraft of locally-based units could be re-deployed elsewhere: the air base and aviation units were in not subordinated, but were separate entities.

2 MRV: k.31, 'Istorija 117. vp za 1968', pp.5-6; MRV: k.27, 'Istorija 5. VaK, 1964-1972', p.32. Personal notes of Colonel Ilija Zlatić that authors received from Zlatić family in 2015.

3 Autor's interview with W/O Steva Miletic, Belgrade March 1997.

4 Hamzić, *Letačke priče*, pp.86-99

5 MRV: k.31, 'Istorija 117. vp za 1968', p.7

6 MRV: k.27, 'Istorija 5. VaK, 1964-1972', pp.94-95.

7 Author interview with Colonel (ret.) Ranko Kovačević, December 2014.

8 Muzej Jugoslavije (MJ): photo collection: 1969_402; MRV: k.31 'Istorija 117. vp za 1969', p.6.

9 MRV: k.31 'Istorija 117. vp za 1968', p.7-9

10 Authors interview with Colonel (ret.) Bogdan Mihovilovic November 2014.

11 MJ: photo collection: 1970_438; MRV: k.31 'Istorija 117. vp za 1969', p.9.

12 MRV: k.27, 'Istorija 5. VaK, 1964-1972', p.23.

13 Hamzić, *Letačke priče*, p.88.

14 Hamzić, *Letačke priče*, pp.88-89.

15 MRV: k.27, 'Istorija 5. VaK, 1964-1972', p.148. Autor's interview with W/O Steva Miletic, Belgrade March 1997. He confirmed to the authors that two Germans landed in light (Cessna/Piper) aircraft. They were taken to HQs in Zagreb, while the plane was ferried out of Bihać by Yugoslav pilot.

16 MRV: k.31, 'Istorija 117. vp za 1969', p.5; Ibid: k.27, 'Istorija 5. VaK, 1964-1972', pp.104-108; Autor's interview with W/O Steva Miletic, Belgrade March 1997.
17 MRV: k.27, 'Istorija 5. VaK, 1964-1972', appendix 15.
18 MRV: k.31, 'Istorija 117. vp za 1971', pp.4-9.
19 MRV: k.27, 'Istorija 5. VaK, 1964-1972', pp.79-82; Ibid, k. 31, 'Istorija 117. vp za 1972/1973', p.5.
20 MRV: k.31, 'Istorija 117. vp za 1974', p.1
21 MRV: k.31, 'Istorija 117. vp za 1972 i 1973', p.6.
22 Author's interview with Captain (ret.) Rajko Lukic 2016.
23 MRV: k.31, 'Istorija 117. vp za 1976', p.7.
24 MRV: k.31, 'Istorija 117. vp za 1977'; Ibid, 'Istorija 117. vp za 1978' and 'Istorija 117. vp za 1979'.
25 Nominally, Nos. 124 and 125 Squadrons were assigned 16 interceptors each (for a total of 32), while No. 352 Squadron had a total of 14 reconnaissance fighters. Of course, the actual number of assigned aircraft varied anywhere between 40 and 50.
26 MRV: k.31, 'Istorija 117. vp za 1972/1973', p.10.
27 MRV: k.31, 'Istorija 117. vp za 1978', p.24.
28 MRV: k.31, 'Istorija 117. vp za 1983', p.XII.
29 MRV: k.31, 'Istorija 117. vp za 1976', p.27-28.
30 MRV: k.31, 'Istorija 117. vp' for period: 1978-1990.
31 MRV: k.31, 'Istorija 117. vp 1980'.
32 MRV: k.31, 'Istorija 117. vp' for period: 1983, 1984, 1985 and 1986.
33 MRV: k.87 'Istorija 352. iae' for period: 1983-1984 and 1987-1989.
34 MRV: k.31, 'Istorija 117. vp' for period: 1982 -1990.
35 MRV: k.31, 'Istorija 117. vp za 1989'.
36 MRV: k.31, 'Istorija 117. vp' 1989 and 1990.
37 Komadna 5. puka VOJIN, pov. br. 268-1 14.05.982; MRV: 'Istorija 5. p VOJIN za 1981 godinu' and 'Istorija 5 puka VOJIN za 1984 godinu'.
38 Komanda 5. puka VOJIN, str. pov. 25-187, 5.12.1975, 'Godišnja analiza obuke', VA, JNA svežanj 6529-1980 'Analiza obuke i vaspitanja 5. puka VOJIN za 1976 godinu'.
39 The AS-74 ATMS was created at explicit Yugoslav request for the purpose of integrating the work of diverse components manufactured by Marconi – foremost the S-600 radar system – with diverse weapons systems in service with the JRV i PVO. As such, it was one of typical modifications created in, for, or by the Yugoslavs during the Cold War.
40 Komanda 5 puka VOJIN, str. pov br 87-48, 12.11.1984.
41 Komanda 5 puka VOJIN, 'Naredjenje za borbenu obuku i vaspitanje u 5. puku VOJIN za 1987 godinu'.
42 Rajica Bošković, *Nebo na dlanu, Vek vazdušnog osmatranja, javljanja i navodjenja*, (Author's Edition, Beograd 2017). pp.474-506.
43 Written Statement of Lieutenant Colonel Mirsad Gadžun, courtesy by Colonel (ret.) Rajica Bošković.
44 MRV: k.27, 'Istorija 5. VaK, 1964-1972', p.25.
45 MRV: k.27, 'Istorija 5. VaK, 1964-1972', p.20.
46 MRV: k.31, 'Istorija 117. vp za 1989', p.10.

Chapter 3

1 Author's interview with Colonel (ret.) Milan Menićanin, February 2015, Zemun.
2 Author's interview with Colonel (ret.) Ranko Krivokapić, 31 March 2015.
3 Author's interview with Lieutenant Colonel Milan Tepšić, 28 January 2015.
4 MRV: k.27, 'Istorija 5. VaK, 1964-1972', p.129.
5 MRV: k.31, 'Istorija 117. vp za 1969', p.1.
6 MRV: k.31, 'Istorija 117. vp za 1984', p.31.
7 MRV: k.72, 'Istorija 200.vb za 1983 godinu'.
8 MRV: k.72, 'Istorija 200.vb za 1983 godinu', p.2.
9 Colonel Dušan Bosković, *Radna beležnica*, (Personal notebook) given to the authors on 18 August 2016.
10 MRV: k.72, 'Istorija 200.vb za 1984 godinu', p.2; Ibid, 1989, p.5.
11 Interview with M. Menićanin.
12 MRV: k.72, 'Istorije 200.vb' for period: 1983 -1989.
13 The large perspex screens used to display situationl information were referred to as "planchettes."
14 MRV: k.72, 'Istorija 200.vb za 1983 godinu'.
15 MRV: k.72, 'Istorija 200.vb za 1984 godinu'.
16 MRV: k.72, 'Istorija 200.vb za 1985 godinu'.
17 MRV: k.72, 'Istorija 200.vb za 1986 godinu'.
18 MRV: k.72, 'Istorija 200.vb za 1989 godinu'.
19 *Instrukcija za upotrebu Objekta Klek*, str. pov, (Komanda RV I PVO, 1968).
20 http://zeljava-lybi.com/forum, (accessed 15 March 2019)
21 http://zeljava-lybi.com/forum (damir vidović)
22 *Instrukcija za upotrebu Objekta Klek*.
23 *Instrukcija za upotrebu Objekta Klek*.
24 *Instrukcija za upotrebu Objekta Klek*.
25 Interview with M. Tepšić; *Instrukcija za upotrebu Objekta Klek*.
26 Interview with M. Menićanin.
27 Interview with M. Tepšić.
28 Interview with M. Tepšić.
29 Autor's interview with W/O Steva Miletic, Belgrade March 1997.
30 Interview with M. Tepšić.
31 Hamzić, *Letačke priče*, pp.90-92.
32 Šetnja kroz podzemni objekt Klek sa pilotom Danijelom Borovićem (04.02.2017.), https://www.youtube.com /watch?v=2g2X-v-8aG8&t=48s> (accessed on 15 March 2019); DVD *Tajne Željave, Vojni aerodrome Željava kod Bihaća*, 2009.
33 Author's interview with Colonel (ret.) Borislav Pejić, 25 December 2014.
34 *Instrukcija za upotrebu Objekta Klek*.
35 Hamzić, *Letačke priče*, 'Letenje' (manuscript).

Chapter 4

1 Interview with M. Menićanin; *Orlovi Plješevice*, br. 7 (1 April 1992), pp.4-5.
2 Interview with M. Menićanin; Author interview with General (ret.) Luka Kastratović, 6 February 2015, Belgrade.
3 Vladimir Rajtar, *Nebeski ratnici, uspomene hrvatskog pilota*, (Vlastita naklada, Zagreb 1995), pp.55-61.
4 Interview with M. Menićanin.
5 Dr Vaso Predojević, *U prodcjepu* (DanGraf , Belgrade 1997), passim; Janez Janša, *Premiki, Nastajanje in obramba slovenske države 1988–1992* (Mladinska knjiga Ljubljana 1992).
6 Interview with M. Menićanin.
7 Interview with M. Menićanin.
8 *Orlovi Plješevice*, br. 7 (1 April 1992), pp.4-5.
9 Author's interview with Lieutenant Colonel (ret.) Branislav Dronjak, 11 February 2015; Author's interview with Colonel (ret.) Dušan Buban, 9 January 2015.
10 Interview with B. Dronjak.
11 Interview with M. Menićanin; Interview with L. Kastratović.
12 Interview with M. Menićanin.
13 Interview with M. Menićanin.
14 *Orlovi Plješevice*, br. 7 (1 April 1992), pp.4-5.
15 Napad na Vaganac 08.10.1991.god. < https://www.youtube.com/watch?v=-xio6u6D3Bs > (accessed 28 May 2019).
16 Interview with M. Menićanin.
17 Interview with M. Menićanin.
18 Branka Primorac, *Perešin, Život i smrt. O Rudolfu, ne samo pilotu…* . (Zrinski: Cakovec, 2001), pp.87-93.
19 Author's interview with Lieutenant Colonel (ret.) Predrag Grandić, May 2015.
20 Primorac, *Perešin, Život i smrt. O Rudolfu, ne samo pilotu*, p.23.
21 Author's interview with Lieutenant Colonel (ret.) Grandic.

22 Aleksandar Radić, *Avion MiG-23 sa našim oznakama, Ratom oblikovana sudbina, Arsenal*, (specijalni prilog magazina *Odbrana*), br. 57.
23 Interview with D. Buban.
24 Komanda 3.korpusa RV i PVO, pov br 25/45-2, 03 04 1992, *Istorija 3.ko RV i PVO 1991*, appendix 7.
25 Interview with M. Menićanin; Author's interview with General Luka Kastratovic.
26 Interview with M. Menićanin.
27 *Orlovi Plješevice*, issues 1-8, December 1991 to April 1992.
28 Bošković, *Nebo na dlanu*, pp.484-506.

Chapter 5

1 Interview with B. Dronjak; Interview with D. Buban.
2 *Orlovi Plješevice*, issues 1-8, December 1991 to April 1992; Bojan Dimitrijević, Milan Micevski, *117. lovački puk, 352.izviđačka avijacijska eskadrila, 200 vazduhoplovna baza* (Galaksija Niš 2015), p.151.
3 Interview with B. Dronjak; Interview with D. Buban ; B. Dimitrijević, M. Micevski, *117. lovački puk*, p.151.
4 Interview with M. Menićanin.
5 Interview with M. Menićanin.
6 Bejdo Felić, brigadir, *Peti korpus 1992-1995*, (Ljiljan, Sarajevo 2002). p.24.
7 Dimitrijević, Micevski, *117. lovački puk*, p.152; Roberto della Croce, *Priča jednog borbenog pilota*, (Stylos Art, Novi Sad 2013), pp.19–40.
8 della Crocce pp.19–40.
9 Interview with B. Dronjak; Interview with D. Buban.
10 MRV: k.25-I, "Istorija VaK 1992", p.36; della Crocce pp.19–40; Sasa Oluić, Goran Antić, Bojan Dimitrijević, *204.lovački avijacijski puk* (VINC, Belgrade 2005), pp.91–92.
11 Interview with B. Dronjak; Interview with D. Buban.
12 Author's interview with Colonel (ret.) Milan Milinković 4 June 2016 Belgrade; Milan Micevski, Bojan Dimitrijević, *83. lovački puk* (Galaksijanis: Niš, 2016) p.136.
13 Interview with M. Menićanin.
14 Interview with M. Menićanin.
15 Interview with M. Menićanin.
16 Interview with M. Menićanin.
17 Interview with R. Kovačević.
18 Interview with M. Menićanin; Interview with L. Kastratović.
19 Interview with M. Menićanin.
20 Interview with L. Kastratović.
21 Interview with M. Menićanin.
22 Felić, *Peti korpus 1992-1995*, pp.19-23.
23 Interview with M. Menićanin.
24 Interview with M. Menićanin; Interview with D. Buban.
25 Interview with M. Menićanin; Interview with L. Kastratović.
26 Felić, *Peti korpus 1992-1995*, pp.65-67.
27 Bošković, *Nebo na dlanu*, pp.484-506.
28 Author's interview with Colonel (ret.) Petko Rašević, 5 May 2016; Bojan Dimitrijević, *Vazdušni rat nad Republikom Srpskom i Republikom Srpskom Krajinom* (Drustvo istoricara Srbije: Belgrade, 2017), p.276.

Acknowledgements:

The authors would like to express their gratitude to Colonel Milan Menićanin (the last CO of the 200th Air Base), as well as other airmen who have served in Bihać and have provided us with valuable personal accounts, including: Major-General Luka Kastratović; Colonels Dusan Buban, Ranko Kovačević, Ranko Krivokapić, Borislav Pejić and Milan Milinković; Lieutenant-Colonels Branislav Dronjak, Predrag Grandić, Milan Tepšić; and Captain Rajko Lukić. Colonel Rajica Bošković and Petko Rašević have helped us to understand the function of aerial surveillance and radar guidance at the 200th Air Base, and deserve our special thanks, too.

Further help was kindly provided by Radovan Cukić from the Museum of Yugoslavia, in Belgrade), Amir Obhođaš and Hrvoje Gržina from the Croatian State Archive, in Zagreb, who selflessly shared precious information and photographs from the archives of their respective institutions, and by Milorad Ristić, who has kindly shared his photographs taken in 1991. Finally, our thanks go to Tom Cooper, who suggested and helped develop this unique project of such importance for the history of Yugoslav aviation during the Cold War.

About the Authors

Bojan Dimitrijević is a historian working as Deputy Director of the Institute for Contemporary History in Belgrade, Serbia. Educated at the universities of Belgrade and Novi Sad, CEU Budapest and University of Bradford, he was the custodian of the Yugoslav Aviation Museum before serving in 2003-2009 as advisor to the Minister of Defence of Serbia, the Minister of Foreign Affairs and to the President of Serbia, and as Assistant to the Minister of Defence. His research into the military history of the former Yugoslavia, and the Balkans in the Second World War, the Cold War, and diverse conflicts since, has resulted in a large number of publications, in Serbia and abroad, including more than 50 books and 100 scientific articles.

Milan Micevski is an entrepreneur from Belgrade. He has been exploring archives and collecting information about aviation history for more than three decades. He is considered one of the leading experts in former Yugoslavia in the field of the Yugoslav Air Force and Soviet Aviation. With Bojan Dimitrijević, he has co-authored seven books related to the history of the Yugoslav Air Force, and has published three additional volumes with two other authors. This is his first instalment for Helion.